# WHO YOU ARE WHEN NO ONE'S LOOKING

# Who You Are When No One's Looking

BILL HYBELS

KINGSWAY PUBLICATIONS
EASTBOURNE

ISBN 0 85476 342 2

Published by
KINGSWAY PUBLICATIONS
Lottbridge Drove, Eastbourne, BN23 6NT, England.
E-mail: books@kingsway.co.uk

Produced for the publishers by
Bookprint Creative Services, P.O. Box 827, BN21 3YJ, England.
Printed in Great Britain

Reproduced from the original text by arrangement
with InterVarsity Press, USA.

# Contents

# Contents

# 1

# *Character*

## Preserving Endangered Qualities

Character—the word is seldom used in the Bible, and we don't see it very often in newspapers or hear it on television. Yet we know what it means, and we immediately recognize its absence.

People who never use the word *character* look around them at junior-high promiscuity, busy abortion clinics and the current epidemic of sexually transmitted diseases, and they mourn the passing of morality. They see elected officials taking bribes, business leaders demanding kickbacks and investors parlaying inside information into untold wealth, and they lament the demise of integrity. Or they read about battered wives, jobless husbands and abused children, and they wonder what is happening to caring.

Character, a wise person once said, is what we do when no one is looking. It is not the same as reputation—what other people think of us. It is not the same as success or achievement. Character is not what we have done, but who we *are*. And although we often hear of tragic lapses of character, describing its absence does not tell the whole story.

**Endangered Character Qualities**

People give evidence of strong character in hundreds of ways every day:

☐ A woman confronts her terror of public speaking so she can tell her church congregation about her miraculous answer to prayer. That's *courage*.

☐ A man vows to get up twenty minutes early every morning to jog around the block, and he keeps his vow. That's *discipline*.

☐ A high-school teacher patiently draws out an inattentive student and discovers she is a gifted writer. That's *vision*.

☐ A college student, overwhelmed by tests and term papers, considers dropping out, but decides to stay and study instead. That's *endurance*.

These four traits are all on my "endangered character quality" list. They aren't glamorous, and they aren't easy. Therefore a lot of people try to get along without them. But strangely enough, the most endangered quality of all is the one that we all think we want—*love*.

Unfortunately, when we say we want the character quality of love, most of us mean only that we want to be loved. We hope people will admire us and treat us affectionately, and we will try to do the same for them. But people of character go beyond the warm fuzzies to the hard work of loving. They do this in many different ways, often without realizing that they are showing strength of character:

☐ A woman refuses to make any more excuses for her husband when he misses work because of a hangover. That's *tough love*.

☐ A man notices his daughter's tear-stained face, and so he sits down and encourages her to tell him what's on her heart. That *tenderhearted love.*

☑ A parent gives up an attractive job promotion so the family can stay in the town where they have made friends and put down roots. That's *sacrificial love.*

☐ A young widow offers forgiveness to the drunken driver who hit and killed her husband. That's *radical love.*

Love, says the apostle Paul, is the most important Christian character trait (1 Cor 13:13), and it is probably the least understood. That is why I have devoted the second half of this book to it. But it is extremely difficult to learn to love unless we also have other character traits: the courage to do what needs doing, the discipline to make decisions and carry them out; the vision to see far into the future and deep into people's hearts; and the endurance to keep going in spite of ridicule, discomfort or simple boredom. That is why I have given the first half of the book to these foundational character qualities.

## Developing a Strong Character

Some people reading the table of contents might be tempted to draw up a chart. "Let's see," they would say, "I'm weak on courage, and so I'll give myself two months to work on that one. Six weeks will probably cover discipline, and I'm sure I can handle vision in two weeks at most. I'll just skip endurance, and that will give me two months on each kind of love. If I follow this plan, in one year I'll have a strong character."

Benjamin Franklin reports in his *Autobiography* that he tried that approach, and it didn't work. As soon as he mastered one good trait and went on to the next, the first one started slipping out of his grasp. Character cannot be developed through good resolutions and checklists. It usually requires a lot of hard work, a little pain and years of faithfulness before any of the virtues are consistently noticeable in us.

Developing character, however, does not have to be a grim task. There are secrets to developing each of the character qualities, and I have shared them in each chapter. More important, Jesus Christ—the only person who has ever consistently excelled in every virtue we could name—offers to develop his character in us as we follow him. This is an offer we can hardly refuse!

## Salvation Is Free

Please keep one very important fact in mind as you read this book: *No matter how wonderful your character is, it will never be wonderful enough to earn God's approval.* This is not a book about how to get God to sit up and notice you or how to improve your heavenly credit rating. As important as character is, it is not a way to earn salvation. That is because salvation cannot be earned—not even by courage, discipline, vision, endurance and love.

Salvation is a gift from the heavenly Father to us. It cost him everything—the death of his beloved only Son. It costs us nothing. Hard work cannot earn it; neither can good behavior or sterling character. The only way we can enjoy a relationship with God is by coming to Jesus Christ, our hands outstretched and empty, and saying, "Lord, I want to follow you. Please take me into your family, scrub me, give me new clothes and make me like you." And Jesus will do exactly that. He will take us as we are and assure us that we are his forever. Then—slowly at first, but surely—he will mold us and shape us until we resemble him.

This book is for two kinds of people. First, it is for you who, whether Christian or not, admire character strength and see the urgent need for it in our society and in yourself. I hope to show you how to get where you want to go. Second, it is for you who, having given your life to Christ, yearn for spectacular transformations and dazzling displays of virtue. I hope to show you that you are already well on the way to character strength, even if the path is humbler than you expected.

Character is our world's most pressing need. If all five billion of us had strong characters, there would be no wars, no hunger, no family breakups, no crime, no poverty. We will not live in such a perfect world until Christ returns and the earth is made new, but, in the meantime, we should not despair. To the extent that our own characters grow stronger, the world will be a better place.

So take courage—a very good place to start.

# 2

# *Courage*

## Overcoming Crippling Fears

**I have** an embarrassing admission to make: I saw *Rocky I* three times. What's more, I saw *Rocky II* three times and *Rocky III* twice, and I even saw *Rocky IV*. I have to admit that each one sent a little tingle up my spine. Not because I think these are especially good movies. They just happen to be about a great subject—courage.

I've always been fascinated by courage. When I was a boy, my dad bought a sailboat in Ireland and sailed it back across the Atlantic Ocean through a hurricane. Before leaving home, he had collected a library of books so that he would know what he was in for, and I read them all. Many of these were books about disasters at sea, and they all included a scene where people were lined up on the deck as the ship went down, wondering what to do because there were not enough life jackets to go around. Some guy would always say, "Here, take mine." As I read that, my breath would get short and my pulse would start to race.

Whenever I hear of someone showing courage instead of cowardice, I find myself saying, "That's what I want to be like." I wish I had more courage. I do not want to be debilitated by fear or paralyzed by anxiety. I do not want to cave in under difficult circumstances and compromise my convictions or give up on difficult challenges. I do not want to be a coward; I want to be courageous. This is a biblical wish, for in 2 Timothy 1:7 Paul says, "God did not give us a spirit of timidity but a spirit of power."

## Courage in the Ordinary

I regret the fact that we usually hear about courage only when someone does some extreme act of heroism that attracts media attention—carrying an old woman out of a burning building, diving into an icy pond to save a drowning child, risking gunfire while dragging a buddy to safety. I love these stories, but they seem bigger than life. Dramatic, once-in-a-lifetime opportunities never seem to happen to ordinary folk like you and me. But the older I get, the more I understand that it takes a great deal of courage to face life's ordinary, everyday challenges.

Every single day we make choices that show whether we are courageous or cowardly. We choose between the right thing and the convenient thing, sticking to a conviction or caving in for the sake of comfort, greed or approval. We choose either to take a carefully thought-out risk or to crawl into a shrinking shell of safety, security and inactivity. We choose either to believe in God and trust him, even though we do not always understand his ways, or to second-guess him and cower in corners of doubt and fear. These choices come our way every day, rapid fire. We face them so frequently that we forget that we are even making them, and we sometimes find ourselves going with the flow instead of

14

carefully making courageous choices.

## Courage to Be Vulnerable

People say that Christianity is for weak people, cowards and quiche eaters. I have always been fascinated by that accusation, because in my experience the exact opposite is true. It takes a great deal of old-fashioned courage to be a Christian. My faith demands the best I have. In fact, a lot of courage is required even to become a Christian. The Bible says that, to become a Christian, you have to own up to your sins before a holy God. That takes courage.

At the beginning of every semester, professors say, "On such-and-such a date, your term paper will be due." But it is easy to get sidetracked with different activities, and when the due date is tomorrow, you suddenly realize that your paper is not ready. You go to the teacher's office and say, "Prof, you wouldn't believe what happened to me. My Aunt Ethel took ill, the library lost the one reference book I most needed and the dog ate the final draft of my paper right after I pulled it out of the typewriter." You say anything but the truth, hoping the professor will be merciful and give you a break.

Probably very few of you ever walked into the professor's office and said, "You made an assignment several months ago. It was fair, and I understood it clearly. Unfortunately, I played too many hands of cards and too much racquetball. I neglected to do what I should have done. I was undisciplined, and I procrastinated. Now I don't have the assignment done. I make no excuses; it was my fault. Do whatever you think is right." Why don't people operate that way? Because it is painful to own up to the truth about our behavior. It takes courage.

When I talk with people about Christianity, I tell them, "You've got to repent before a holy God. You have to tell him the truth about yourself—that you've lied, you've hurt people, you've

15

cheated; you've been greedy, dishonest, unfaithful to your spouse, self-centered." When I say that, I see terror in their eyes. They do not want to be that open and vulnerable. They shift in their seats. They look at their watches and wonder how to get out of such confrontation.

What is going on? Inside them, a voice is saying, "Confession would be painful and humiliating, and it would make you feel uncomfortable and exposed, but it's the right thing to do and you have to do it." At the same time, another voice is saying, "Don't look at yourself that closely. Take it easy. Go with the flow. Cover your tracks."

Too many people cave in to their fears and say, "I just can't do it. It would be too embarrassing, too humiliating." So they say ridiculous things like "Who, me, a sinner? No, not me. Harry's awful, and Mary's wicked, but I've lived a pretty good life. I may have made a few minor mistakes in judgment—nobody's perfect—but not many, mind you. Nothing serious."

When I hear that kind of response, I have a strong urge to say, "Pal, you're gutless. You know what you should do, but you're too chicken to do it. You don't have the guts to tell God the truth about who you really are. You're afraid of the pain, the embarrassment. You're too frightened to admit the obvious." I also want to add, "If you're too chicken to repent, then please don't ever say Christianity is for weak people. Apparently it's for people with more courage than you have." If it takes courage to *become* a Christian, it takes even more courage to *be* a Christian.

## Courage to Follow

We used to play a game at summer camp in which we would blindfold one of the kids and have him or her run through a wooded area, relying on a friend for verbal directions to help navigate. "Turn to the left; there's a tree coming!" "There's a log in front of you—*jump!*" Some kids would not trust the verbal directions whatsoever. They would shuffle their feet and walk very slowly, even though their friends were shouting that the way was clear. Other kids would trot along, and a few would go like gangbusters. All the kids, though, had to fight the urge to tear off the blindfold so that they could see what was ahead. It takes a great deal of courage to follow another person's lead.

As Christians, we sometimes feel like those blindfolded children. Paul says in 2 Corinthians 5:7, "We walk by faith, not by sight." We are not alone in the woods, though—God "shall direct thy paths" (Prov 3:6 KJV). But following Jesus Christ demands an enormous amount of courage. Quite often his leadings sound illogical, irrational, countercultural. Sometimes he is so challenging that I say, "No, I think I'll just crawl back into my shell and play it safe." Then a voice inside me says, "Where's your courage, Hybels? Get up and walk. You can trust God."

Cowards do not last long on their spiritual pilgrimages. They shrivel up and disappear. It takes enormous courage to repent and become a Christian. It takes enormous courage to follow God's leadings in the Christian life. Some of his callings demand the best that you can summon. Some of his tests stretch you to the limit. Some of his adventures evoke great fears and doubts. Truly, spiritual courage is on the endangered character-quality list.

## Relational Courage

Another kind of courage is also in danger of extinction today—*relational courage*. I try not to give two-cent answers to hundred-dollar questions, but when people ask me what it takes to build a meaningful marriage, I say, "courage."

For a marriage relationship to flourish, there must be intimacy. It takes an enormous amount of courage to say to your spouse, "This is me. I'm not proud of it—in fact, I'm a little embarrassed by it—but this is who I am." It also takes courage to look your spouse in the eye and say, "Our marriage is in serious trouble, and we've got to do something about it." What do most people do? They put their problems on the back burner and go their own directions. While they pursue their own careers and their own recreations, the marriage disintegrates from lack of courage. They did not have the courage to put on the gloves and say, "Let's fight for this marriage. Let's go to a marriage retreat. Let's see a marriage counselor. Let's get together with another couple we respect. Let's lay it out on the table and solve these problems instead of running from them." It takes courage to fight off the "greener grass" temptations, to work through layer after layer of masks, cover-ups and defense mechanisms, to keep working on that marriage year after year. Relational courage does not apply only to the husband-wife relationship. It also takes courage to raise kids. How often I see parents backing off from proper discipline because they don't want to endure their kids' disapproval! The kids throw a tantrum and say "I hate you," and the parents give in. If you want to raise your children the way God wants them raised, you will have to let the little tyrants get mad. Show some courage and say, "You don't intimidate me, little one. This is the right thing to do, and this is what you're going to do."

It also takes relational courage to build significant relationships with friends, to look another person in the eye and say, "Isn't it time we stopped talking about the weather and the stock market and started talking about what's going on in your life and mine? Isn't it time we became brothers?" Not many men have the courage to challenge each other, to fight for each other's spiritual and relational growth. But I have learned over the years that I will never be a success in my marriage, with my kids or with my friends, without courage.

## Courage to Be Moral

We could discuss many other kinds of courage—vocational courage, courage to face difficult circumstances, moral courage. How much courage must you summon to operate ethically in the marketplace? What kind of guts does it take to be honest? We don't want to offend customers, and so we say, "The shipment will be there Monday," when we know it won't leave the warehouse until Wednesday. We want people to think we are honest, and so we say, "I report all my income" when in reality we have a drawerful of unreported check stubs at home. April 15 is a great day to separate courageous people from cowards, because that is when moral courage hits us in the wallet.

How much courage is required to stay sexually pure in a sex-crazed culture? How much is required to stick to a conviction when everyone at the office, at school or in the neighborhood says, "You're hopelessly idealistic, old-fashioned, and a little bit strange—in fact, you're a religious fanatic"?

## How to Grow in Courage

But how do you become courageous? Do you make a wish? Say a prayer? Wave a wand?

You grow in courage when you *face your crippling fears.* Sometimes we think courageous people were born without fear. In actuality, courageous people are ordinary people like you and me who began at some point to face their fears rather than running from them.

When I was growing up, my dad saw that I was a timid guy, and so he always challenged me to do things I was afraid to do. When I was in grade school, for example, he'd take me down to our produce company and bark out, "Billy, go out and back in that semi." I'd been driving tractors for several years, but I'd drag myself into the cab of that forty-foot rig just shaking with fear. Sometimes it would take me forty-five minutes, and the truck would be half-jackknifed against the dock. But when I crawled out, my knees shaking, Dad would say, "Good job." The next time he would ask me to do it, it would be just a little bit easier.

Sometimes when Dad and I were in our sailboat on Lake Michigan, coming in between two cement piers with huge waves tossing the boat one way and then the other, he would say, "I've got to go down below—you take over the helm." I knew exactly what he was doing: waiting until I was terrified out of my mind, and then putting me in control. One minute the boat would be heading right toward one cement barrier, and the next minute a wave would pitch it over to the other side. About the time I eventually managed to get the boat where it belonged, Dad would come up and say, "Now that wasn't so bad, was it?" The next time it was a little bit easier.

Dad treated me the same way when I was learning to fly. Meigs Field is one of the most dangerous airports in the United States. Right off the lakefront in downtown Chicago, it is surrounded by water and has high crosswinds. So, of course, whenever we flew to Chicago on business from Kalamazoo, my dad would make me land at Meigs Field even though several other airports were available. But every time I did it, it got a little easier.

Every fear that is faced and overcome becomes a building block. Each success gives you a new sense of confidence. You grow in courage as you face your crippling fears. You also grow as you *surround yourself with good models*. The Bible says, "Bad company ruins good morals" (1 Cor 15:33). If you spend time with spineless people, you will probably become spineless yourself. Unfortunately, we are often surrounded by people who cave in, quit, compromise and play it safe as part of their daily routine. But if you want to grow in courage, make a calculated choice to increase your exposure to courageous people. Read autobiographies of courageous people; articles about courage; and Bible stories about people like Moses, Daniel, Esther and Paul who, though petrified, went ahead in faith and grew.

Finally, you grow in courage as you *allow your mind to be*

*transformed.* Sooner or later you begin to understand the centrality of courage in all walks of life. Courage is not an isolated, optional character quality. It is not merely a nice trait for people who want it but unnecessary for those who are not interested in it. Courage is foundational to being a Christian.

It takes courage to begin a walk with Christ, to reach out your hand and trust him. It takes courage to lead a life of obedience to Christ. It takes courage to be moral and to build significant relationships with your spouse, your children and with your friends. It takes courage to expand a business, change your major or start a new career. It takes courage to leave home or to go back home.

Courage—we all need it, and God wants us to have it. "God did not give us a spirit of timidity but a spirit of power." But you cannot sit still and expect courage to come and find you. You have to go after it.

# 3

# *Discipline*

## Achieving Success through Delaying Gratification

**Some people** seem to succeed at everything they try. They have successful careers; they relate well to their families; they may be involved in church and community activities; they are active, growing Christians—they are even physically fit. When you get close to people like this and try to determine just how they manage to fulfill so much of their potential, you find that in almost every case one quality plays a significant role—*discipline.*

By contrast, other people have an embarrassing string of setbacks, disasters and failures. If you get close to them, and if they are honest with themselves and with you, they will probably offer you a candid appraisal of why these calamities have befallen them. "Well, you know, I just started to let things slide," they may say. "I put off doing my homework." "I neglected to follow up

23

leads." "I didn't keep my eye on the store." "I didn't push my chair back from the bar." "I stopped making my calls." "I didn't watch the till." "I didn't take care of myself." "I didn't spend time with my family." "I thought problems would solve themselves." The list of reasons for failure could go on and on, but most of them stem from one conspicuous lack—*discipline.*

Discipline is one of the most important character qualities a person can possess. It plays a key role in developing every area of life. But how many highly disciplined people do you know? Can you quickly think of five people that are truly disciplined in all areas of their lives? Are you disciplined yourself? God has given me hundreds of acquaintances, and only a small fraction of them demonstrate discipline to a significant degree. Not that people do not want to be disciplined—they do. But discipline, I fear, is an endangered character quality.

In various polls, I have asked people what character quality they would most like to have more of; usually one of the top responses is discipline. But there is a great deal of confusion as to what discipline really is and how to practice it. People do not know how to develop greater levels of discipline and put it to work for them in everyday life.

What, then, is this thing we don't understand but want more of? I can give you a two-word explanation of this confusing character quality that defines it, captures its essence and uncovers what is really at its core. These two words are easily remembered—you can think about them during the day and use them in your conversation. Discipline is *delayed gratification.*

## First, the Bad News

According to Scott Peck in his book, *The Road Less Traveled,* "Delaying gratification is a process of scheduling the pain and pleasure of life in such a way as to enhance the pleasure by meeting and experiencing the pain first and getting it over with."

He adds, "It is the only decent way to live." I couldn't agree more.

Did you ever watch a normal, well-adjusted, blossoming, disciplined boy eat a piece of cake? He carefully carves around the frosting and eats the cake part first. When he gets done with that, his eyes get a little bit bigger and he attacks the frosting. It's the only decent way for a kid to eat cake. For that matter, did you ever watch an adult eat Neopolitan ice cream? Usually vanilla goes first, then strawberry, then chocolate. Well-developed cake- and ice-cream eaters know how to increase their satisfaction by using the principle of delayed gratification.

It takes continual parental prompting over a period of years before most children learn to use this principle, but those who mature properly eventually learn that they will not enjoy dinner and after-dinner activities if they have homework hanging over their heads or if they know the dog needs a bath. That is why well-disciplined students attack their responsibilities—their schoolwork and chores—as soon as possible after school. Once these tasks are finished, they can enjoy the rest of the evening.

As people move out of adolescence into adulthood and the job market, they usually knowingly and of necessity enter the work force near the bottom rung of the ladder. They willingly put up with long hours, short vacations, repetitive tasks and minimal pay because they know that, if they endure the entry-level discomfort for a while, the payoff will eventually come in the form of more flexible hours, higher pay, longer vacations, more responsibility, more interesting tasks. They are practicing delayed gratification: purposefully scheduling the pain early, trusting that a much more enjoyable phase will result. This principle, which works well in the job market, can be applied to many other situations as well.

For example, delayed gratification is important to spiritual life. As a pastor, I have often heard people say, "I've learned something over the years. If I discipline myself to spend ten or fifteen minutes early in the morning in a quiet place getting a proper perspective on my walk with the Lord—writing down some thoughts, reading my Bible, listening to a tape, praying—the whole rest of my day seems much more satisfying." Listen closely to what these people are saying. If I roll out of the sack while the house is still cold and invest my time and energy on something worthwhile, then the rest of the day will be better. This is delayed gratification as it pertains to the spiritual walk.

## Delayed Gratification in the Family

Discipline also pertains to the relational life. Married couples who understand the value of discipline say to each other early in their relationship, "Let's work very hard on this marriage right now. Let's face all our conflicts as they arise. Let's not let things slide. Let's do whatever it takes right now to make our marriage mutually satisfying." This may require a lot of hard work, and it may be uncomfortable or even painful at times, but it brings wonderful results in the form of more fulfilling and satisfying days ahead.

Sometimes my wife, Lynne, and I get together with couples who are experiencing pain in their marriage. After talking with them we often realize that, even if they have been married twice as long as we have, they are just now dealing with things that we took care of during our first two or three years of marriage. As problems arose or conflicts surfaced between them, they would refuse to face them. It was too uncomfortable, and so they pretended nothing was wrong. Rather than endure present discomfort for the sake of future happiness, they let things slide. The result of their lack of discipline, of course, was escalating discomfort that eventually became intolerable. They would have been much better off saying, "Let's go through the pain right now so that we'll have a longer time of pleasure ahead."

Delayed gratification is also important in training children. A lot of parents are unwilling to make the sacrifices that are necessary in order to meet their children's deepest needs. A promotion at work, a TV show, or a nap on the sofa may all seem much more enticing than playing Candy Land with a three-year-old. There's no question about it: it is hard to devote yourself wholeheartedly and regularly to bringing up your children properly. But hard work during the children's early, impressionable years usually forms strong characters in them. Parents who discipline themselves to do this, trusting God for the strength to keep going, are likely to enjoy the payoff of a lifetime of solid relationships with their children.

## No Pain, No Gain

Achieving good physical condition is impossible without discipline and delayed gratification. People make a calculated decision to forgo certain culinary ecstasies because they want good news at weigh-in time. The delay is worth it when they look at themselves in their new slacks in front of the full-length mirror. At the health club where I work out we say, "Why do we do these things? Because it feels so good when we stop." There's some truth to that. When you take the pain for forty-five minutes or an hour, you feel better about yourself. Your muscle tone is good. You feel alert. You enjoy satisfaction that lingers all day and into the night.

It's the same thing with handling finances. If there is any area where delayed gratification must be practiced, this is it. You experience pain or discomfort when you make a conscious choice not to spend money on something you would really like to have, but as your nest egg grows and your investments mature, you say, "I did it the right way."

Discipline is not hard to understand, then, if you can remember the words *delayed gratification*. But understanding discipline and practicing it are two different things. The key to practicing discipline can be described in three words—*advance*

27

*decision making.* Here's what I mean.

## Advance Decision Making

Once you make up your mind that the only decent way to live is to schedule the pain and the tough challenges first so that you can enjoy the pleasure, the rewards, and the payoff later, then you have to take an important practical step. You must make advance decisions as to *how* you are going to practice discipline in the various dimensions of your life.

For instance, physical health is a dimension that is very important to me. I come from a family with chronic heart problems on both sides. Two uncles on one side and two uncles on the other had heart attacks and died before they were fifty. My dad died at fifty-three. And trouble started showing up in my medical reports when I was fifteen. So, for me, there is no playing games with my health. I know I need to do something about it.

I understand intellectually that I must first endure the pain of running and weightlifting if I am going to experience the satisfaction of feeling well and being healthier. That is, I *understand* discipline. But understanding alone is not enough to improve my health; I must put my beliefs into practice. I *practice* discipline when I make the decision, in advance, that Monday through Friday at 3:30 I will leave the office and go to the health club to work out.

I made that decision several years ago, and I regularly write it on my calendar. Still, every day at about 3:15 my body starts sending signals: "You don't want to work out today. You're a little sore down here, a little tired up there. You're awfully busy in your work. You really don't want to leave now, do you?" A big part of me does not want to work out, you see, and so we start this little argument.

"Yeah, well, I should go."

"Oh, but you can skip a day now and then. After all, you don't

28

want to turn into a fanatic."

So goes the debate. If every day at 3:30 I made the decision whether or not to go work out, I would not work out very often. When it came right down to the moment of packing up and leaving, with all those emotions and voices converging on me, I would probably cave in most of the time. But I practice advance decision making. Because I have already decided to go to the club, I ignore arguments against going, no matter how persuasive they may sound.

"Sorry," I say to my body, "I'd like to hear you out, but I can't do anything about it. It's already been decided. It's on my calendar. You're not going to reverse the decision. It's done." My body may groan, but it gets itself to the weight room. Advance decision making has become a powerful way to implement the practice of discipline in my daily life.

## Money Mastery

Advance decision making works in financial planning just as well as in maintaining physical health. Lynne and I put our family budget together at the beginning of each year. We pray about it, we agree on it, and we put it down on paper. Then we covenant together—that is, we make an advance decision—to abide by our budget, come what may.

Payday comes, and what happens? "I saw the most wonderful lamp. It has our name written on it. And it's on sale." We start smiling at each other. "It would look perfect on that little table, and it would make the room so much brighter. We really *need* it." Without an advance decision about our budget, we would probably run out and buy that lamp right then. But because we have agreed to live by our budget, we look at the figures and ask, "Is it in there, or isn't it?" If it isn't, that's too bad; the decision has already been made. We don't fight about it or try to backtrack. We live by it.

## Personal Relationships

Advance decision making is extremely important in one area where, sadly, it is rarely applied—relationships. If a husband and wife, for example, are going to continue to nurture their relationship and grow, they need at least one night a week of interaction time alone. Lynne and I call it our *date night*. For several years I have been encouraging the married couples of our church to take weekly private time together. Almost everybody agrees that the idea is good, even essential. Few couples actually do it on a regular basis, however. I am convinced that the people who stick to it every week, month in and month out, have made the advance decision to do so. They have a standing appointment with each other, and a regular babysitter comes in at a prearranged time so that they can keep it. It's all arranged in advance; so when the time comes, they do it.

Most important of all, advance decision making is an important factor in our relationship with God. We know we are saved by grace and not by hard work or planning or discipline. Our spiritual life is God's gift to us, just as our physical life was given to us with no effort on our part. But without practicing discipline, we will not grow spiritually any more than we would grow physically if we neglected the disciplines of eating, sleeping and exercising.

If you have any interest whatsoever in fulfilling your spiritual potential, it is essential that you begin to practice advance decision making in your spiritual life. I have discovered three things that I must do if my spiritual life is going to flourish. First, I need to participate regularly in worship services at my church. Second, I need a daily time of personal interaction with the Lord. Third, I need fellowship with other believers in some type of Christian service. If I do not actively participate in these three endeavors, I wilt. I feel spiritually frustrated, and it seems as if God is not using me. Sooner or later every true believer comes to an under-

standing of what it takes for him or her to flourish as a Christian—
the minimum daily or weekly requirements of a healthy spiritual
life. And this is where discipline enters in.

When you determine what has to happen on a regular basis for
you to flourish in Christ, it is time to make some advance decisions. If in order to grow spiritually you need to be part of the
body of Christ when it gathers to worship, make an advance
decision to be there—and go. Say, "All right, I *will* be with the
body of believers when it assembles. I *will* attend church every
Sunday morning." Don't wait until Saturday night when you get
in late and then ask, "Do I feel like setting the alarm?" Don't ask,
"Who's speaking? What's the message about?" Don't look out the
window to see what the weather is like. Go because you have
already decided to do so.

In the same way, if you need personal time with the Lord each
day, find the time, block it off on your calendar, and keep the
appointment. Perhaps you have your devotional time when you
get up in the morning, when you arrive at your office, during your
lunch hour or before you go to bed at night. You might spend
the time reading the Bible, praying, writing in your journal or
listening to a tape—anything that strengthens you in your walk
with the Lord. Structure your time and activities in whatever way
best suits your needs, but do not leave your time with the Lord
to chance. Make the advance decision to keep your daily appointment with him, and keep it without fail.

## Sticking with Discipline

When you come to the point in your spiritual life of saying, "I'm
going to harness the powers of discipline and commit myself to
meeting my minimum requirements," you are really saying, "I'll
do what it takes. I'm willing to go through the discomfort and
pain of the investment stage first so that I can experience the
blessedness of flourishing as a Christian the rest of my life." You

are making an advance decision to delay gratification as long as necessary to achieve the results you most desire. That's discipline.

The essence of discipline, then, is delayed gratification, and the key to practicing discipline is advance decision making. But some of you are saying, "I can't do this alone." You heartily believe in delayed gratification and you have frequently tried advance decision making, but your efforts fall short. Somehow your high resolves melt in the heat of temptation or the pleasant warmth of laziness.

Good news—God does not expect you to do it alone. He knows you need brothers and sisters running along with you (in fact, that's one reason Christians come to God as a church and not just as individuals). If you need help in sticking to your decisions, harness the power of *accountability*. Ask two or three friends to hold you accountable for your decisions. Tell them, "I've made these advance decisions because I really want the payoff. Please hold me to them." This is a tremendous boost to discipline. In addition, God says in his Word that the Holy Spirit helps you produce discipline in your life (Gal 5:23). You can depend on his aid.

## What's in This for Me?

Discipline without rewards would eventually seem rather grim. Fortunately, the payoffs of a disciplined life are enormous. Chicago Bears linebacker Mike Singletary is a member of my church. I have been to his home and I have seen the impressive collection of training equipment he has set up in his basement. "Mike," I said, "the Bears have tens of thousands of dollars worth of workout equipment at Halas Hall. Why do you want more in your basement?"

"I want to go overboard," Mike told me. "I'm willing to pay any price, because, when game time comes, I want to be ready." That's why, after a full day of practice, Mike often goes home, walks down to his basement and continues to work out. What are the payoffs for him? Being able to play pro football; playing in the Super Bowl; being named all-pro for three seasons.

Discipline will bring payoffs in whatever area of life you apply it. The payoff for spiritual discipline is a stable Christian life— maturity, usefulness, satisfaction, contentedness. The payoff for relational discipline is a flourishing marriage and family life along with a network of significant relationships. The payoff for physical discipline is a fit body, increased energy, resistance to sickness, lower insurance rates, higher concentration levels and increased self-worth. The payoff for financial discipline is freedom from debt and the satisfaction of knowing your little nest egg is growing.

The rewards of discipline are great, but they are seldom immediate. When the world clamors for instant gratification and easy solutions, it is hard to choose the way of discipline instead. But you will never build a walk with God, a marriage, a body or a bank account by obeying the world's law of instant gratification. Payday will come in its own time, if you endure the pain and put your nose to the grindstone now.

*Delayed gratification. Advance decision making. Accountability.* These six words define discipline and tell how to achieve it. The rewards of a disciplined life are enormous, and they are within your reach if you are willing to make the effort. Which area of your life most needs discipline? When are you going to take the first step?

# 4

# *Vision*

## Looking beyond
## the Obvious

**The story** is told of two prisoners in one small cell with no light except what came through a tiny window three feet above eye level. Both prisoners spent a great deal of time looking at that window, of course. One of them saw the bars—obvious, ugly, metallic reminders of reality. From day to day he grew increasingly discouraged, bitter, angry and hopeless. By contrast, the other prisoner looked through the window to the stars beyond. Hope welled up in that prisoner as he began to think of the possibility of starting a new life in freedom.

The prisoners were looking at the same window, but one saw bars while the other saw stars. And the difference in their *vision* made a huge difference in their lives.

A business leader told me that, in his opinion, there is a shortage of visionaries entering the marketplace. "There are lots of nuts-and-bolts people in business these days," he said, "people who will do exactly what they're told to do, exactly the way they're told to do it—no more, no less. There are plenty of robots, but precious few idea people. We need people with imagination, people who think overtime, who find ways to make improvements or increase efficiency."

A church leader called me long distance to see if I could suggest the name of a pastor who might be available to lead his congregation. He made it very clear that he did not want someone who would simply come to the church and preserve the status quo. "We are looking for a pastor with vision," he said.

A single woman told me not long ago that she was praying that God would lead her to a man who, in her words, "really knows where he is going, who is willing to take risks, who will keep me guessing." In other words, she wanted God to find her a visionary. "But," she sadly said, "I'm not sure there are many of those around anymore." I wanted to tell her she was being overly pessimistic, but I couldn't. There are a lot of nuts-and-bolts people who will do exactly as told, and there are a lot of people firmly committed to preserving the status quo, but there are not many visionaries around anymore.

## Why Are Visionaries Hard to Find?

Vision is on my endangered character quality list along with courage and discipline. The reason is simple: it takes too much work to be a visionary. It's much easier just to go with the flow and do what's expected. It takes courage to break out of conventional thought patterns. It takes confidence and daring to risk failure with a new idea or a new approach. Visionaries tend to fail many times before they ever succeed, and most people feel too fragile to take risks. They would rather be safe and secure.

It also takes a lot of old-fashioned perspiration to be a visionary. It takes discipline to sit down with a pencil and paper and vow not to get up from your desk until you come up with five new ways to do something, three new ways to improve something or two new options for salvaging something that is in danger of disintegrating. It takes endurance to get on your knees and stay there until God supernaturally ignites a fresh thought in your mind. It takes hard work to plan for what could happen in six months, a year, three years or five years in your business, family, marriage or ministry. It probably won't ever happen anyway, so why dream? It's a lot easier to see bars than stars.

Many of us seem to think that dreams, grandiose plans, inventions and creative bursts are reserved for writers, physicists, composers and artists. They are not for ordinary people with ordinary vocations, ordinary families and ordinary relationships. But I think that God disagrees with that kind of thinking. I think he would say that vision, like courage and discipline, is a character trait that can be stimulated and developed in anyone who is willing to understand what it really is and then to work hard at making it part of everyday life. Everyone can choose to look at bars or at stars. In fact, everyone makes that choice several times every day.

## Seeing Solutions

Vision can be defined in many ways; I offer three definitions covering three aspects of this important character quality. First, *vision is the God-given ability to see possible solutions to the everyday problems of life.* Visionary people are solution oriented, not problem oriented. There is a tremendous difference between those two approaches.

In Luke 16:1-9 Jesus tells a parable so unusual that many teachers would rather turn the page and go on than try to understand it. It is the parable of a crooked accountant (traditionally, an "unjust steward") who used creative bookkeeping techniques.

His boss eventually caught on and decided to give him his termination notice. But while the accountant still had a few days left to work, he said to himself, "I have a problem. I'm going to lose my steady paycheck. I'm too old to dig ditches and too proud to panhandle. I'm going to have to solve this somehow."

So the accountant did an unethical but ingenious thing: he called some of the people who owed his boss money. "How much do you owe us?" he asked.

One man answered, "A hundred measures of wheat."

"I'll tell you what," the accountant said. "Change your copy of the invoice, and I'll change mine. Put down that you owe us only fifty measures."

"Well, thanks," said the man. "That's a very nice thing for you to do. If you ever need a favor, call me up."

"Don't worry," said the accountant, "I will." Then he called another debtor, and another, and repeated his generous offer.

What was the crooked accountant doing? Plainly, the man was using the company's capital to build up a reserve of personal favors so that when he lost his job he would be able to find another one. His boss quickly saw what he was doing, too, and he had a most unusual reaction—he praised his accountant's ingenuity and shrewdness!

Now neither Jesus nor the boss ever praised deceitfulness, dishonesty or creative bookkeeping. But both of them recognized the accountant's vision. When faced with a serious problem, he did not hide, blame somebody, run to the bottle or jump off a cliff. Instead he faced his problem and came up with a shrewd way to solve it. Jesus commended him because, as soon as he saw his problem, he became solution oriented.

What is so mind boggling about that? Doesn't everybody become solution oriented when faced with a pressing problem? Strangely, no. The longer I work with people, the more I realize that the prevailing tendency is not to try to solve problems but to get stuck on them. A person is going along happily when suddenly he is hit with a big problem—work related, marital, family, relational, financial, spiritual, physical, whatever. His first reaction is to wonder, "Why me? Of all the billions of people on this planet, why did this problem hit me?" He begins to moan and groan about the fact that he now has a problem.

It is not enough just to feel bad about the situation; he is soon calling his friends to see if they will moan with him about his bad luck. He gets on his knees and tells God about the problem in vivid detail, as if God didn't know what was going on. He turns it over and over in his mind like a piece of meat on a rotisserie, eventually sending out formal invitations to a black-tie pity party. Before he knows it, his whole life is revolving around his problem. Paralysis sets in. He has chosen to let his problem define him, and he can no longer either solve it or attend to business in other areas of his life. He *is* his problem.

Amazingly, he has done everything he can about his problem except the one thing he should do—devote himself doggedly and determinedly to finding a solution to it.

## All Things Are Possible

The disciples once thought that they had heard Jesus say that respectable, well-to-do, upstanding community leaders could not be saved. If that were true, then their chances of being saved were not very good either. The disciples, who had not yet become visionaries, immediately gave up hope. They saw no solution; salvation was obviously out of reach. Jesus looked at them and said, "Fellas, you're right. With human beings, some problems have no solutions. But with God all things are possible" (Mt 19:26).

Does your problem seem bigger than life, bigger than God himself? It isn't. God is infinitely bigger than any problem you ever had or will have, and every time you call a problem unsol-

39

vable, you mock God. "With God all things are possible." Visionary people face the same problems everyone else faces; but rather than get paralyzed by their problems, visionaries immediately commit themselves to finding a solution. Almost as a reflex reaction to the problem they say, "The situation is bad, all right, but no problem is bigger than God. And right now, before I get bogged down, I need to start down the path of solving it." More often than not, visionaries find a way, with God's help, to deal with their problems and overcome them rather than surrender their lives to them.

Vision is a vitally important quality to cultivate, because life is really just a series of problems, challenges, trials, and disappointments. If you allow yourself to be overwhelmed by difficulties, your future is not bright. You will get stuck first on one problem and then on another. You will spend your whole life spinning your wheels and cursing the mud. If, on the other hand, you cultivate vision—if, whenever you are faced with a problem, you immediately explore ways to deal with it—you will not only avert all sorts of discouragement, but you will also discover just how much creativity and wisdom God wants to give his children who look to him for help. How often we underestimate God, doubting his ability to assist us with the everyday problems of life!

Some years ago a woman talked with me after a church service. I knew she had been despondent about something for a long time, and so I probed a little bit until she said, "You know, I am sick and tired of my job."

"What are you doing about it?" I asked.

"Well, there's just nothing that can be done," she said.

"All right," I said, "let me give you a homework assignment. Go away to a quiet place. Take a pencil and paper and put down five possible solutions to your job dilemma." To get her started, I gave her two of the five off the top of my head. I remember the look in her eyes as I did this—a mixture of defiance and shock.

This woman had been surrendering to her problem for so long that she had forgotten that she could do something to solve it.

## Four Steps toward Problem Solving

"Well," you may say, "obviously Hybels hasn't walked in my shoes. If my problems could be solved that easily, I would have done so right at the beginning." I admit I am not in your shoes. I don't know your boss, your wife, your child, your friend, your doctor. Like you, however, I have some mountain-sized problems that, humanly speaking, are unsolvable. But I don't want pity parties, and I don't want to get stuck on my problems. So by God's grace and with the help of a lot of other people, here is what I do when I face a problem. These four practical steps may also help you when you face problems that look unsolvable.

First, I repeat Matthew 19:26: "With men this is impossible, but with God all things are possible." I have known that text for a long time, but I have to apply it to each new problem that comes my way. When a solution looks impossible, that truth flies right out the window. I have to haul it back and hang on to it tenaciously. God is bigger than my problem.

Second, I go to a place where I can be all alone, and I take another Scripture verse at face value. James 1:5 says, "If any of you lacks wisdom, let him ask God, who gives to all men generously and without reproaching, and it will be given him." I force myself to believe that God will fulfill that promise in my case. If I cannot believe it right away, I pretend. I say to myself, "I'm going to act as if that promise is true." I say to God, "I'm going to take a walk, and I'll keep walking until I have some sense that you've heard my prayer for wisdom, until I know you're going to help me find a solution to this problem." Sometimes the walks are long, but eventually I believe.

Third, I meet with brothers and sisters in Christ who are solution-oriented people. I don't want to meet with people who

41

will just sympathize. "Poor Bill, what a terrible problem he's facing." That does not help me much. It feels good for a while, but the next day I wake up and the problem is still there, big as life. So I meet with people who can tell me how they have solved similar problems in the past.

Fourth, in a spirit of humility, prayer and openness to the Holy Spirit, I list what look like the four or five best possible solutions to my problem. Then by faith I start down the path of one of those possible solutions, trusting God to close some doors and open others, unveil more possibilities or cause something to break in the situation until my problem is solved. I often tremble as I take those first steps, but I would rather move ahead in fear than stay stuck in a bad situation.

No matter what kind of problem you have—relational, marital, financial, spiritual, emotional, vocational—you can find a solution if you are willing to be visionary. Claim the promise that all things are possible with God. Ask him for wisdom. Discuss your situation with wise friends. Put down some options, and head out by faith. It will make a tremendous difference in your life to be on the road to a solution.

## Seeing beneath the Surface

Vision is not only for problem solving, of course. A second definition of vision is this: *Vision is the ability to see beneath the surface of people's lives.* Visionary people know that it pays to look beyond the obvious to understand what makes other people tick.

Most of us are amazingly gifted at seeing the obvious in one another. "He's arrogant (or talented, or selfish, or vain)," you say, and your friend says, "I've noticed that too." You smile agreeably at each other and remark about your marvelous mutual insight. But all you have seen is the obvious. Visionary people don't settle for the obvious—that's too easy for them. They look beneath the surface for the other person's uniqueness. They look at the heart, the character, the hopes and the fears that motivate the person's behavior.

Jesus showed vision when he changed Simon's name. All that everybody else ever saw of Simon was his impulsiveness, his aggressiveness, his faintheartedness. But Jesus looked beneath his outer layer and saw a potential that no one else saw. Simon had backbone, a strength that even Simon himself didn't know he possessed. So Jesus renamed him *Peter,* which in Greek means "rock" or "pillar"—something suitable for the foundation of a tall building. "On this rock," Jesus said, "I will build my church, and the powers of death shall not prevail against it" (Mt 16:18). Can you imagine the shock on the faces of the other disciples when Jesus said that? But Peter did indeed become a pillar (Gal 2:9), a respected leader and a founder of the church in Rome. His leadership career goes back to Jesus' vision, his willingness to look beneath Peter's surface-level characteristics to his true self.

I love Proverbs 20:5: "The purpose in a man's mind is like deep water, but a man of understanding will draw it out." There is greatness in the hearts of all people who are created in God's image, but someone with vision has to find it and draw it out.

Visionaries have an important mission to accomplish in the lives of others—looking past the obvious into the shadows, trying to draw out the greatness that God himself put there. We need visionary *parents*—mothers and fathers who will study their children diligently, pray intensely and converse with them perceptively in order to identify and draw out each child's uniqueness. We need visionary *spouses.* Most of us spouses have a stranglehold on the obvious. We need to look beneath the surface and probe around until we find the jewels hidden deep in our mate's soul.

We need visionary *business leaders* who will treat their workers like real people and diligently try to match their unique skills

43

with commensurate responsibilities. In the church, we need visionary *disciplers*, mature Christians who can look past the stumblings and bumblings of baby believers and say, "I see potential there, and I'm going to draw it out." We also need visionary *witnesses* who can look at unbelievers with no time for Jesus and say, "I wonder what Christ's transforming power could do in that person's life?"

This vision that looks past the obvious and sees what's really going on in people's souls can be developed. It takes time—time for meaningful meditation on people's character, thoughtful conversations, persistent prayer for insight and quiet reflection. It also takes courage, for the Holy Spirit may lead you to affirm something in that person that no one else sees.

## Seeing As God Sees

I am going to offer a third definition of vision that is more difficult for me to formulate because it is on the cutting edge of my own walk with the Lord. I am not sure how this works, and I do not always know how to activate it, but I know this kind of vision is important. *Vision is the God-given ability to catch a glimpse of what God wants to do through your life if you dedicate yourself to him.*

God once came to Moses and said, "I need a leader to perform a vital, but difficult, task for my people."

Cowering, Moses said, "Here I am, Lord—send my brother. He's the gifted one. He's impressive. He can speak in public." At that point in his life, Moses had no vision of how God could use him.

I have to admit that I share Moses' problem. I look in the mirror and say, "I'm not the kind of guy that God does miracles through." My life is not earmarked for greatness. There is no aura of drama about it. I feel plenty ordinary most of the time, and I often wonder if I matter at all.

But every once in a while—and I won't pretend that it happens often—when I'm in tune with the Lord, the Holy Spirit seems to whisper to me, "Hybels, take your blinders off. Where's your vision? You're not much, but God is. And you matter to him. Why don't you believe what you preach? God delights in using foolish people to confound wise people. He loves to use weak people to amaze strong people. And he'd love to use you, if you'd just believe all things are possible."

At some time in your life you must have sensed God saying to you, "I want to use you in a significant way. It's time to start going in a new direction. I want you to change vocations (go back to school, quit school, start a ministry, strike up a friendship, track down an opportunity, get a job, go to the mission field), because you matter to me. I have great plans for you, and I'm going to work in your life. If you'll just take those blinders off, I'll use you." Just for a moment you felt a flutter in your heart, and you thought, "Maybe that was God's voice." But then instead of looking at stars, you focused on bars. In front of those metallic reminders of reality, you turned off the voice. You quenched God's Spirit. You said, "I think I'll stay in my cell." And God was grieved.

I cannot ask you to do something that I am not willing to do. I want to be more willing to say, "God, here I am. Use me. Lead me. If you have something significant planned for my life, count me in. I'll follow you the best I know how—trembling, but trusting. I want to see stars, not bars. I want to grow in vision."

# 5

# *Endurance*

## Crashing through
## Quitting Points

**Looking back** over the last ten years of your life, what do you wish you had not quit?

Do you wish you had finished high school, college or graduate school?

Do you wish you had kept on taking voice lessons, dance lessons, piano lessons or skiing lessons?

Do you wish you had stayed with that rather low-level job that nevertheless had a great deal of potential for advancement?

Do you wish you had continued to work on your relationship with your first spouse?

Do you wish you had maintained that long-term friendship that dissolved when the going got rough?

Do you wish you hadn't given up on God?

Most of us try not to think about our failures any more than we have to, and Scripture itself advises us not to live in the past (see, for example, Phil 3:13-14). But occasionally it pays to consider the high cost of quitting. So many people live with scars or lingering wounds from having quit on something or someone. So many look back on their lives, shake their heads and ask, "Why did I cash in so easily?"

The answer is obvious: it is infinitely easier to quit than to endure. It's easier to go out and play than to practice scales. It's easier to watch TV after work than to take night classes at the community college. It's easier to walk out of the room during an argument than to stay and work through the conflict. It's easier to read the paper and drink coffee in your bathrobe on Sunday morning than to get yourself and your family up, dress everybody, face the traffic and go to church. It's easier to do what you want to do with your life than to kneel before God, turn the reins over to him, and wait patiently and expectantly and sometimes agonizingly for him to lead you. It's easier to quit following Jesus Christ than to go through the painful process of daily surrender.

We may as well admit it—it's almost always easier to quit than to endure. But quitting exacts a high cost, and many of us have paid dearly for giving up too soon.

## Grand Prize: Endurance

Imagine that the Illinois State Lottery, during Easter week when people are supposedly thinking more about Christ than about money, offers a character quality instead of a few million dollars as the grand prize. The ticket lines at convenience food stores are shorter than usual, but still thousands of people pay their dollars and guess at the winning numbers.

When the time comes for the winning number to be announced, eager radio listeners and TV watchers from all over the state hear that a forty-four-year-old, balding store clerk from Joliet has won the fully developed character trait of endurance. And he—we'll call him Herman—comes forward and pretends to be excited, and for about two days he is the object of TV cameras and reporters' questions, and then he goes back to work at K-Mart and is completely forgotten.

Let's check in on Herman ten years later and see how he has fared. Ask him about his grand prize, and see him smile broadly and say, "You know, I wouldn't have believed it at the time. In fact, I was rather angry that the one time I guessed the right numbers, I got a character quality instead of a check for seven million dollars. But I was forty-four years old and still working for minimum wage because I could never keep a job. I guess I always wanted instant promotion and instant money, and whenever a job got tough, I'd quit.

"But ever since I was given endurance, things have been different. I've stayed at K-Mart for ten years, doing my best work wherever I've been assigned, and they've moved me up the ladder several times. Now I'm assistant manager. I went back and finished my high-school education by spending two years at night school. I never could have done that before—I would have quit after the second class. But I kept going because now I have endurance, and I'm real proud of that diploma. And I also put endurance to work in my marriage, which was almost washed up when I won the lottery, and my wife and I have been getting along just fine for several years now. I had just about given up on God, too, but I started my search all over again and I now have an exciting spiritual life. I feel good about myself for the first time in my life, thanks to endurance."

Herman cannot talk much longer because he is being paged over the K-Mart intercom, but he concludes the interview by saying, "Looking back on it, I see that a seven-million-dollar check would have enabled me to keep on quitting whatever I wanted to quit. It probably would have destroyed my dignity and maybe even my life. But this thing called endurance—now that has turned me into a successful, happy person."

## The Instamatic Era

James 1:12 says, "Blessed is the man who endures trial, for when he has stood the test he will receive the crown of life."

We spend a lot of energy trying to avoid trials, but we actually ought to thank God for them. Adversity helps us develop endurance, and endurance is a powerful weapon to have in our character arsenal.

But endurance makes my endangered character-quality list along with courage, discipline and vision, because we live in the instamatic era. Nowadays we demand overnight stardom, overnight success, overnight growth, overnight solutions, overnight marital bliss and even overnight spiritual maturity. If our expectations are not met overnight, we have a strong tendency to quit. This is especially true for those of us under forty-five. We were called the "now generation" in the sixties, and things have not gotten any better since. So we quit jobs, educational programs, relationships and spiritual quests—prematurely. Even if we are Christians, we give up on God's mission for our lives before we've really put it to the test. We are fast becoming a weak-willed people, because we don't understand endurance. But endurance is essential for facing life's challenges.

Endurance sustains *courage*. A burst of courage for fifteen minutes is good, but it is not enough to carry you through. Endurance gives staying power to *discipline*. It is important to understand delayed gratification and to make advance decisions, but these are not one-time actions. Endurance turns your *vision* into reality. Without it, visions are no more than pipe dreams. Endurance is one of the most essential character traits of all, but you will never win it in a lottery. You can't buy it, and you can't bargain for it. How, then, can you develop it?

## Quitting Points

*You build endurance by learning how to crash through quitting points.* If you're a runner, you know what a quitting point is. It happens on the twentieth lap when your sides are splitting, your legs are heavy, your throat is burning and your mind is screaming "Quit! Enough! Don't go another lap, another half lap, even another step!" You're at a physical quitting point.

It happens in a work situation when the pressure is mounting as a deadline draws near. You are dizzy from working as hard as you know how, and suddenly the boss comes in and barks yet another assignment. You think, "That's it! I can't stand it one moment longer. I'm going to write out a resignation notice, throw it on his desk, and walk out." That's a vocational quitting point.

It happens in an argument with your spouse for the tenth time over the same thing. The two of you strongly disagree; frustration has been building for weeks. Then your spouse says the magic word that ignites the fireworks. Your emotions go through the roof. Everything in your mind and body screams, "Quit, storm out, call the lawyer—it's not worth it anymore." That's a marital quitting point.

It happens in your struggle to build a good character. You have been wrestling with a particular sin, and someone you care about makes fun of your ideals. Why continue to struggle, you wonder, if nobody else even cares? Why not just cave in to the prevailing morals of the day? That's a moral quitting point.

It even happens in your walk with God. He has been at work in your life, and you have experienced important changes. You know that he is leading you down the right path, but he is making some enormous demands and you don't know if you can trust him—or yourself. "Nobody else is doing this," you think. "Am I the only one crazy enough to trust God down a blind alley?" Then you experience failure, human rejection or scorn, and you say, "That's it, God. I'm not going a step further. You're asking more than I can give." That's a spiritual quitting point.

## Sweet Relief

There are many other kinds of quitting points—educational, emotional, psychological, relational. In almost everything you do, you will reach a point where all you can think of is the sweet relief of cashing it in. In our grandparents' day, quitting was considered disgraceful. But today, it's often praised.

Perhaps endurance does not make good drama, but my blood boils when TV glamorizes giving up. Watch the screen—things are tense at work. The employee is disagreeing with the boss. Nerves are snapping as the background music builds. The camera comes in tight on the employee and shows the veins popping out on his forehead. A moment of silence, and then his voice proclaims, "I quit!" The music crescendoes wildly as he storms out, slamming the door behind him. And while the show's sponsors sing the praises of beer or antacids, viewers across the nation sigh and say, "That's exactly what I want to do to my boss someday. I want to quit in living color, in front of a vast audience, with violins and a drum roll."

Look again—a husband and wife are disagreeing. The tension builds. At the peak of anger, the wife suddenly slaps her husband across the face, just as the cymbals crash, of course. Spinning on her heels, she storms out and slams the door just as the employee did on the last show. And half the wives in America say, "That's what I want to do. Johnny, get the pie tins and we'll go talk to Dad. This time I'm going to tell him to take a walk."

Watching these shows, we do not stop to think that the man is now unemployed, the woman is divorced and little Johnny doesn't have a dad anymore. All we see is the glamour, the sweet relief of cashing it in and walking out. But God's truth pierces through our tinsel-town values. He says it's the other way around. "Blessed is the man who endures" (Jas 1:12). "He who endures to the end will be saved" (Mt 24:13). The lights and music should not be focused on those who quit but on those who, when they think they cannot go one step further, grit their teeth and say, "With God's help I am going to press on." That is when the heavenly choirs break into singing and the spotlight from above shines down. That is when ordinary people like you and me become extraordinary in God's sight.

You may not feel a lot of slaps on the back in those moments. You certainly do not hear the angels sing or feel the burning spotlights of heaven. But if you are walking with the Lord, you hear the Holy Spirit whisper the words, "Blessed are those who draw on God's strength, who endure trials and crash through quitting points—for they shall receive the crown of life."

## Crashing Through

If you are at a quitting point right now, count the cost very carefully before throwing in the towel. Quitting is not glamorous. It does not develop your character. God does not call it blessed. In most cases, you will regret it the rest of your life. But when you come to the quitting point and then, drawing on God's strength, crash through it, you build endurance in your life.

You may be at a quitting point in your job. You wanted overnight satisfaction, advancement and fulfillment, and you did not get it. Do you seriously think you will find these things somewhere else? One of my colleagues said to me last week, "I'm sure there have been at least fifty times when I've wanted to leave this place. I'm grateful that, by God's strength, I didn't do it, because I'm now experiencing more blessedness, more fulfillment, more excitement than I ever dreamed possible. I'm glad I stayed."

Or you may be about ready to give up on your marriage. I am embarrassed to admit it, but early in our marriage that sometimes became an inviting option to me—and Lynne was not to blame, believe me. Fortunately, God was gracious. Other people encouraged us to work on our problems, and the Holy Spirit worked overtime inside us. Now our marriage is well worth all the adjustments, pruning, chipping and molding God had to do. Sometimes I look at Lynne and say, "Oh, God, I would have been a foolish man to cash in our marriage!"

Perhaps you are at a spiritual quitting point. You have attended church for a number of weeks, months or even years, and it still is not clear to you who Jesus Christ is. You still wonder why, when you pray, no one seems to be listening. You still wonder why you don't feel what everyone else claims to feel. Yet God's Word says that "he exists and that he rewards those who seek him" (Heb 11:6). "You will seek me and find me; when you seek me with all your heart, I will be found by you, says the LORD" (Jer 29:13-14). Those promises apply to you.

Or perhaps you have walked with God for many years and are tired of struggling, tired of trying to conform your life to Christ's, and tired of the responsibility and the pain of leadership. How attractive it looks to slip back into automatic pilot and become a spectator instead of a leader or a servant. But do you really want to cash in the influence you have on other people's lives, the opportunities you have to serve for God's glory?

You may even be at so many quitting points that you are thinking about ending your life. But suicide is not the answer. God is bigger than any problem you face. The solution is to find out just what path he is going to open up so that your life can take a new course.

Whatever your quitting point, I challenge you to test God's truth and faithfulness by saying, "God, I am going to proceed, trusting you to empower me to crash through this quitting point and come out in one piece on the other side."

## Brick or Tissue Paper?

Endurance is a precious quality to me. It has helped me through countless times when I have felt pressed to the wall, tempted to give up my ministry and go back into the marketplace. Because endurance means so much to me, I assign myself extra-credit projects that help strengthen it.

When I run laps at the gym, I always decide in advance how many to run. When I reach my goal, I am usually tired and aching and at my quitting point. That's when I often say, "I'm going one more lap. This quitting point is not made of brick; it's made of tissue paper, and I'm going through it."

When I'm at the beach on vacation, I like to windsurf. I'll go out and back over and over again until my arms are burning, my legs are aching and I'm ready to drop from exhaustion. That's when I say to myself, "I'm going to turn around and go back out just one more time." Again, I want to prove to myself that quitting points are made of tissue paper, not brick.

When I'm working on sermons I sometimes get to the point of saying, "That's it! My mind is scrambled, and I can't come up with one more new thought." That's when I take a walk around the church building and resolve, "I'm going to sit down once more, and that quitting point will prove to be tissue paper."

Every time you break through a quitting point, you prove to yourself that quitting points are not as solid as some people think they are. With God's help you can go through them more often than not. Every time you break through one, a victory is gained in heaven and in your life. Endurance has grown stronger in your spirit. The next time, even if the mountain is higher, you will have more endurance to help you climb it.

Quitting points are painful—Jesus knows that even better than we do. He endured all the way to the cross. Every time the soldiers plucked his beard or someone slapped his face or the whip tore his back open, all hell screamed, "Quit!" When the nails went through his hands, bystanders ridiculed him and he couldn't feel his Father's presence anymore, his whole soul screamed, "Quit!" But by strength from above and by his own resolve, Jesus Christ the Savior crashed through his quitting points and died the death that makes salvation possible for every human being.

I'm glad we follow a Savior who "for the joy that was set before him endured the cross" (Heb 12:2). I'm glad that endurance, even though it will never be offered by the state lottery, can be developed. And I'm glad the Holy Spirit says to us every time we come to a quitting point, "Crash through it—I'll give you the strength. It's made of tissue, not brick."

# 6

# *Tender Love*

## Walking in Someone Else's Moccasins

**A huge plant** in our living room got a disease, and my wife, worried that it would infect other plants in our house, decided to dispose of it. One morning while the children were at school she hacked all the branches off and loaded them in garbage bags. She left the big pot with the plant's stump in the living room so that, when I got home, I could carry it out to the garage.

In the afternoon our kids went into the living room and saw the pot. Our son, who was then six, burst into tears. "Why did you do such an awful thing?" he asked Lynne. "Did you have to kill the plant? Did it hurt when the plant died? Did it bleed? Couldn't you have called a doctor?" It took half an hour for Lynne to explain the situation and put him back together again.

Meanwhile our daughter, age nine, said disgustedly, "Todd, it

57

was only a sick old house plant. Don't worry about it. I'm glad Mom chopped it down and put it out of its misery. Are you going to chop down any more, Mom? Do you need any help?" Two children born of the same parents, raised in the same family with the same levels of love—but one was being a lot more tender than the other.

Some friends of mine had a dog that had been a loyal, faithful member of the household for thirteen years. But the pet's health had deteriorated so much that the only kind thing to do was to put her to sleep. The family agonized over having to do that. They postponed the evil day repeatedly. Eventually all the members of the family except the dad had to go out of town for some occasion, and he decided to take the dog to the vet. He told me, "I picked the dog up and carried her out to our car. As I drove to the vet's office, she crawled up on the seat, put her head on my leg and nuzzled me. It was terribly hard to take her into the office. After the vet put her to sleep, I went back out to the parking lot and sat for a while before I could go back to work."

The man and his brother worked together. When he walked into the office, his brother asked where he had been. "Well, you know, today was the day," he said. "I had to take the dog to the vet to be put to sleep."

His brother responded incredulously, "You paid a vet to put the dog to sleep? You should have brought it to me. I would have knocked it over the head and taken care of it—no problem." Two brothers with the same parents and similar upbringing, but one is tenderhearted and the other is very tough in spirit.

## Some Tender, Some Tough

Paul says in Ephesians 4:32: "Be kind to one another, tenderhearted, forgiving one another, as God in Christ forgave you." For many of us, that is not an easy command to follow. Tenderness seems to be a reflex reaction to some people, but for others it is alien and difficult. You see this in public places like airports and shopping centers. An elderly woman is struggling with luggage or packages, and a steady stream of able-bodied people pass her by. Some even scowl and say, "Get a move on, Grandma." And then a tenderhearted person comes along and takes time to help her.

In the parable of the good Samaritan, Jesus pointed out that being religious is no guarantee of being tenderhearted (Lk 10:30-37). The priest and the Levite passed the injured traveler on the other side of the road because they did not want to get involved. But an irreligious man, a Samaritan, gave assistance because he had a tender heart.

There are many reasons why some people are tender while others are tough. Part of it can be explained as God's workmanship. He makes us all different. Part of it is due to family heritage, the individual's temperament and the kind of experiences he or she has had. Both tenderness and toughness are important character qualities; both are necessary sides of love.

I offer this chapter to the Rambo clones—people who, like me, are naturally on the tougher end of the continuum. I want to show you that some softening has to happen in your life, that you need to learn to be kind and tenderhearted if you want to have a character like Christ's. But the next chapter is dedicated to the gentler Christians who need to learn about tough love—speaking the truth even when it hurts, making waves in relationships that should not stagnate, rebuking people before they shipwreck their lives. The tough need to learn tenderness, and the tender need to learn toughness. Both are important aspects of Christ's love.

## The Tough Guy's Dilemma

If we harder-hearted Christians are honest, we have to admit that our tough approach can do damage. We kid people that we shouldn't kid, and when they get hurt we say, "Can't you take a joke?" We don't listen to other people very well. Usually while they are talking to us we are either making unrelated plans or mentally responding to what they are saying. We wonder why many people are so weak and timid. We use people and dispose of them unceremoniously when they have served our purposes. Although we may not realize it, others tell us we act superior. We love to be right, to compete and especially to win. If the truth were known, we secretly view tenderhearted people as emotional weaklings or psychological misfits. We don't understand them.

But in our moments of quiet reflection, which come semiannually, if that often—and usually only when we've been brought low by a financial setback, an accident, an illness, a divorce, or some other crisis—we don't like what we see in our souls. This is especially true if we are in a saving relationship with Jesus Christ. During my own rare times of introspection, I have asked myself, "How can my heart be so hard? I've experienced the personal love of Jesus Christ firsthand. His love has marked my soul and changed me. I know the Holy Spirit resides in my life and is working me over from the inside out, trying to make me a more loving man. I know that God has graciously put me in charge of a community of brothers and sisters who are growing in their attempt to become more loving people. But I'm still too callous and cold. What more is required for me to become tenderhearted? What practical steps can I take to relate to people in a more tender fashion?"

## Distorted Vision

Shortly after becoming a Christian, I realized I needed a lot of softening. I needed help in becoming kind, gentle and tenderhearted toward others. One day while reading the Bible, I ran across an episode in Jesus' life in which he healed a blind man. Usually when Jesus healed people, he just touched them or spoke to them and their ailment was cured instantly. But in the story told in Mark 8:22-26, the healing had two phases. Jesus touched the man's eyes, and then he asked, "Do you see anything?"

The man replied, "I see men; but they look like trees, walking." Jesus touched him again, and this time he received his whole sight. At last he could see people clearly, without distortion.

In those days I did not understand much about biblical interpretation, but I knew that story spoke to me. I feasted on the words, "I see men; but they look like trees, walking." I thought, "That's my problem too. I don't see men very clearly. People, as far as I'm concerned, are just part of the landscape. They are about as important to me as trees."

I remember saying to myself, "When I look around and see other people, I don't think, 'Wow, this person is a custom-designed creation of the almighty God. He has God's image stamped on him. He is the object of God's greatest affection. Jesus shed his blood for him. The Holy Spirit is seeking him out night and day in order to bring him into a relationship with the Father. He really matters to God.' I don't think like that. For me, people are like trees, walking." And when I realized how far my view of people was from Jesus' view, I knew I needed my vision changed. I needed to learn to see people as they really are.

## Seeing with God's Eyes

I know a lot of hardhearted people. They tend to be on the fast track. They are going places and getting things done. The adrenaline races through them. They have goals to achieve, quotas to meet, deals to be cut. What they are doing seems so important to them that they view people primarily in relation to themselves and their own projects and aspirations. People are either necessary means to their ends or unnecessary obstacles hindering the way of progress. To a hardhearted, fast-track person, people are either tools to be used or trouble to be avoided.

Hardhearted people, then, tend to divide the world into

winners and losers, heavyweights and lightweights, survivors and basket cases, sharp and two bricks short of a load. It is hard for them to realize that they have never bumped into just an ordinary person—that every living, walking, breathing human being is an extraordinary treasure in God's eyes. It is hard for them to grasp that losers and basket cases matter to God every bit as much as winners and survivors; that Russians, Cubans, Libyans and Palestinians are just as important to God as Americans; that God loves prisoners, homosexuals and bag ladies as much as he loves stockbrokers, dental students and seminarians.

All human beings are God's beloved creations, and all are invited to receive forgiveness at the cross. Because God has invited everybody into his family through Christ, every person we meet is a potential brother or sister. When we grasp this truth and begin to see people for what they mean to God, we begin to soften up and treat people tenderly.

Hardhearted people, pay attention. Next time you're rude to someone because he or she is only a waitress, only a parking lot attendant, only the butcher or baker or candlestick maker—stop! There are no "only's" in God's eyes. These people may be doing humble work, but each one is extraordinary to God. Each one matters. Employers, if you have to give an employee a pink slip, don't just "sack" her. Remember that she matters to God. Single people, if you feel you should break up with the person you are dating, don't just "dump" him. Remember that he matters to God. Drivers, next time someone shakes his fist at you in traffic, don't snarl back. Remember that even hotheads matter to God. And God's treasures should be treated tenderly.

## Feeling with God's Heart

To learn tenderness, then, we hardhearted people need first to begin to see as God sees. Second, we must make ourselves walk a mile in the other person's moccasins. Tenderhearted people have a natural tendency to empathize with others, to feel what they are feeling. Hardhearted people, by contrast, can look at people who are hurting, broken or upset and say, "They seem to be having a problem." It is much easier for them to analyze other's problems than to feel with them.

A few years ago, Lynne and I went to see *Sophie's Choice,* a rather heavy psychological drama, a part of which was set in a World War 2 extermination camp. I was a barrel of laughs that evening. Feeling like a teen-ager on a date with the prettiest girl in school, I bought popcorn, put my arm around my wife and settled back to enjoy the movie.

About three-quarters of the way through, the movie started to get intense. Holding her two children in her arms, Sophie was having to decide which one to hand over to the Nazi officer for sure incineration. "This is pretty heavy drama," I thought. "But it's getting a bit long. I wonder if the popcorn stand is still open? I'd like another box." As I turned to look, I noticed that Lynne was sobbing. I decided to get popcorn some other time, and she cried through the rest of the movie.

As we walked back to the car, I could tell that it was no time for cracking jokes. So we drove home quietly and went to bed without saying a word. I did not know what was wrong with her until a day and a half later when she was finally able to bring herself to talk about it. "I want to tell you why I was so upset," she said. "I was picturing having Todd in one arm and Shauna in the other, and having thirty seconds to choose which one was going to live and which one was going to die. How in the world would I ever make that choice?" Lynne had not only put on Sophie's moccasins; she had crawled into her socks, her dress and her bonnet. She became Sophie for a while.

This did not happen to me. I stayed outside the characters' skins and watched the drama unfold; in fact, I did not immediately understand why my wife was so powerfully affected by the movie. Empathy does not come naturally to us hardhearted people. We have to slow down and make a determined effort to put ourselves in other people's shoes. We need to ask ourselves how it would feel to be in their situations.

How would it feel to be handicapped, unable to stand up, walk, dress yourself, drive or even find a good seat in church because there is no room for your wheelchair?

How would it feel to be unemployed, to have mortgage and car payments you cannot make and to have children you cannot provide for?

How would it feel to be Black in a White community that is not particularly sensitive to minorities?

How would it feel to be divorced, to be widowed, to lose a child or a parent?

How would it feel to have cancer, multiple sclerosis, Alzheimer's disease or AIDS?

When we take the time to empathize, to walk a mile in someone else's moccasins, a few cracks begin to appear in the concrete that surrounds our hard hearts.

## Treating People As Christ Treats Us

Of course, tenderheartedness has to go beyond feelings. It's vital to start seeing people as God's treasures. It's important to learn to empathize with them. But how should these feelings be expressed? Should I slobber all over people? Should I give away the store? Should I sell my house and join the Peace Corps? What does a tenderhearted Christian do?

In a nutshell, Scripture says to treat people the way Jesus Christ treats you. When you pray, the Lord listens attentively to every word you say. Why not treat your spouse, your children, your friends and your coworkers the same way? Slow down, turn off the television, close out any distractions and say, "I'm going to listen, because I really want to hear what you have to say." When you make a mistake, Jesus lifts you up, forgives you, and continues to treat you with love and respect. Why not do the same for the people with whom you live, work and worship? When you feel lonely and insecure, the Holy Spirit stays by your side, comforts you and assures you of God's love. Why not give comfort and support to the people you love when they are going through difficult times?

No believer ever has to doubt God's affection. Open the Bible and find evidence of it on every page. "You are precious in my eyes, and honored, and I love you" (Is 43:4). "I have called you friends" (Jn 15:15). "I am with you always, to the close of the age" (Mt 28:20). "As a father pities his children, so the LORD pities those who fear him" (Ps 103:13). If God does not want his children wondering whether or not they are loved, why not express your own affection regularly so that your family, friends and coworkers know how you feel about them?

What will happen if we hardhearted people begin to see people as they are in God's eyes, walk in their shoes and treat them the way Christ treats us? The results will be unbelievable. After their initial shock, our spouses and children will go wild with joy. Our coworkers will shake their heads and say, "The whole atmosphere around here has changed—I wonder what has happened to old Harry Hardheart?" Our superficial friendships will deepen into warm brotherly or sisterly relationships. Our churches will multiply in effectiveness as people discover they can find love where Christ is worshiped.

Thank God for people who are naturally tenderhearted. Without them our lives would be barren and unfulfilling. Thank him also that we can all grow in tenderness—even those of us who are naturally tough.

# 7

# *Tough Love*

## Insisting on Truth
## in Relationships

**Who said the** following harsh words?

"Woe to you, teachers of the law and Pharisees, you hypocrites!"

"You blind guides! You strain out a gnat but swallow a camel!"

"You clean the outside of the cup and dish, but inside they are full of greed and self-indulgence."

"You are like whitewashed tombs, which look beautiful on the outside but on the inside are full of dead men's bones and everything unclean."

"You snakes! You brood of vipers! How will you escape being condemned to hell?"

You probably recognize these words of Jesus, the gentle Shepherd, the tenderhearted, meek and lowly Savior (Mt 23:13-33

NIV). How could he talk so tough to people he claimed to love? Why did he say these hard words?

Jesus said these things because they were true. His words were upsetting, difficult to receive, tough to swallow—but true. Quite often the truth must simply be told straight out, with no room for confusion or misinterpretation, to avoid the greater damage of living by lies. Jesus had an overwhelming concern for the people he was addressing. He loved them, and he wanted them to come to grips with the truth before they shipwrecked their lives and jeopardized eternity. Jesus was demonstrating *tough love*—a kind of love that is usually painful but very potent.

I've received my share of hard words over the years:

"Billy, head on down to your room. There's no supper for you tonight. Mistakes are one thing, but lies are another."

"The next time you talk to your mother like that will be on the way out the door to shop for an apartment."

"You know I love you, but I'm not going through with this wedding. You aren't mature enough."

"Do you call this a marriage? I call it a joke, and I'm not going to let you continue to treat me like yesterday's mail."

"Why do I feel I can't disagree with you? Are you always right?'

I could go on and on. There comes a time when the truth must be told, and it must be told straight. Fortunately, some people have loved me too much to allow me to continue to act in a rebellious, deceitful or arrogant fashion. So they rolled up their sleeves, took me to the woodshed and made me face some unpleasant things about myself that were damaging my character and jeopardizing our relationship. That's what I mean by tough love—and I love those people for using it on me.

## Tender People and Tough Love

Tender love is badly needed in this hardhearted world. We need compassion, sensitivity, affirmation and encouragement. But without its counterpart, tough love, tender love can rapidly degenerate into a sniveling sentimentality that paves the way for deception and, eventually, the disintegration of the relationship.

To tenderhearted people, tough love sounds unnatural, frightening and maybe even unchristian. It admittedly comes easier to those of us who are by nature tougher hearted. When we see a problem in the life of someone we love, we do not hesitate to go to work on it. We easily say, "What we need here is surgery. So let's lay this guy out and, with a scalpel or a dull butter knife—it doesn't matter which—let's hack through his surface-level excuses and get right to the heart of the matter. And if it causes a little bleeding, that's okay as long as the problem gets fixed. We'll stitch him back up later. If he survives the surgery, he'll thank us later."

Tenderhearted people who read that last paragraph already have their stomachs in their throats. They are saying to themselves, "Surgery? Scalpel? Blood? I never want to see that happen to anyone, let alone do it myself. All I want is peace and harmony. Maybe with enough hugs, the problems will solve themselves and the pain will go away." To you tenderhearted people, God would say, "I understand your tender spirit—I made you that way. But if you're going to learn how to really love, you're going to have to learn about tough love."

## Who Needs Tough Love?

One of my colleagues is a true-blue charter member of the tender hearts club. He says he knew nothing about tough love until recent years when some of his Christian brothers demonstrated tough love to him in a lot of ticklish areas in his life. Several months ago, hearing I was preparing a sermon on tough love, he wrote me this note: "Tell those tenderhearted people that if my brothers hadn't demonstrated tough love to me, I wouldn't have a growing relationship with my wife, an effective ministry, a disciplined walk with Christ, a righteous hatred of sin, respect for the people I lead, my debts paid and money in the bank. But because of tough love, I have all those things. Everybody needs tough-love lessons."

Everywhere I look I see people who need to experience tough love—precious people who really matter to God but who are running around and around in circles, dizzied by deception. I see married couples on the edge of serious trouble, young people pushing their luck to the limits, all kinds of people wandering aimlessly in the wastelands of destructive pleasure seeking. Too many of us who see these people destroying themselves simply chew our nails and wring our hands, saying nothing because we do not understand tough love.

But somebody has to get close to these people and tell them they're on a merry-go-round going nowhere. Somebody has to shake them and say, "God has a better way for you. Get off the merry-go-round and look to him for direction." Somebody has to say, "I love you too much to watch you shipwreck your life, your marriage, your family, your job, your soul. So sit down and listen to me, because I'm going to say some hard things to you. I don't like doing this, but I must because these things are true and because I love you too much to stay silent when I see you hurting yourself."

In order to understand tough love and express it effectively, a person must have two fundamental convictions. First, he or she must believe that *truth telling is more important than peace keeping.* Second, he or she must realize that *the well-being of the other person is more important than the current comfort level in the relationship.*

## Truth Telling or Peace Keeping

Tenderhearted people will go to unbelievable lengths to avoid any kind of turmoil, unrest or upheaval in a relationship. If there's a little tension in the marriage and one partner asks the other, "What's wrong?" the tender one will answer, "Nothing." What he or she is really saying is this: "Something's wrong, but I don't want to make a scene." In choosing peace keeping over truth telling, these people think they are being noble, but in reality they are making a bad choice. Whatever caused the tension will come back. The peace will get harder and harder to keep. A spirit of disappointment will start to flow through the peace keeper's veins, leading first to anger, then to bitterness and finally to hatred. Relationships can die while everything looks peaceful on the surface!

Peace at any price is a form of deception from the pit of hell. When you know you need to tell the truth, the evil one whispers in your ear, "Don't do it. He won't listen. She won't take it. It will blow up in your face. It will cause too much hurt. It will only make things worse. It's not worth it." If you believe those lies, there is a high probability that you will kill your relationship sooner or later.

The Lord gives a command in Ephesians 4:25 that makes tenderhearted people tremble to their bones: "Therefore, putting away falsehood, let every one speak the truth with his neighbor, for we are members one of another." First, we are to stop lying to each other. Second, we are to speak the truth—"in love," Paul says in verse 15. It takes courage to speak the truth when we know that doing so will make waves and rock canoes. But any approach other than truth telling, over time, will undermine the integrity of our relationships. A relationship built on peace keeping won't last. Tough love chooses truth telling over peace keeping and trusts God for the outcome.

## Counterfeit Peace

In the early years of our marriage, both Lynne and I chose peace keeping over truth telling. I was starting up a church and I had a lot of upheaval at work—no money, no people, no buildings and plenty of disagreement among those who were involved with the project. Lynne had troubles of her own at home. She was pregnant; we had two boarders living with us who took a great deal of her time; and she was teaching flute lessons to help make ends meet. So with upheaval at home and upheaval at work, we had a common understanding whenever we got together— "Don't make any more waves." Nevertheless, inside us the frustrations were building up.

God began to work on Lynne's heart. Before long, my tenderhearted wife started meeting me at the door saying, "Sit down, I have to tell you something. I haven't been truthful with you. I am sick and tired of being tenth on your priority list. You don't show me much affection. I don't like the way this marriage is heading, and I'm not going to stand for it."

I did not respond very well. I did not say, "I'm glad to hear what's on your heart. I'll change my schedule and start thinking about your needs as well as my own." Instead I yelled, "With all the problems I have trying to start this church—and you lay this trip on me! What do you want, anyway? Here, take some blood."

In spite of my reaction, Lynne stuck to her guns. She knew our marriage needed work, and she decided to fight until I saw the light. Over the years God used Lynne's tough love until I faced the truth about myself and allowed him to do a lot of surgery on me.

But then, once I started listening to Lynne and working on my problems, I began seeing some things in her I did not want to live with anymore. Having learned the value of truth telling, I decided to open up. "Sweetheart," I said, "I see a streak of self-centeredness in your life that bothers me."

Sweet, softhearted Lynne did not say, "Thank you for sharing your feelings." Instead she ran away sobbing, "I can't believe you'd say that!" and slammed the bedroom door. But I stuck to my guns, and we had several more rough months. Eventually she made some changes, just as I had had to do, and our marriage became peaceful once again. But this time there was a difference. This was not a counterfeit peace based on avoiding the real issues. This was the peace of the Lord—based on truth, real and lasting.

## Well-Being or Comfort

To love as Jesus loves, then, you have to put truth telling ahead of peace keeping. You also have to put the other person's well-being ahead of the comfort level of your relationship.

Imagine a mother looking out the living room window at her three-year-old son, who is riding his Big Wheel in the driveway. Her heart spilling over with love, she goes to the kitchen, pours a glass of lemonade and takes it out to him. After he drinks it, she picks him up and hugs him and tells him how much she loves him. The little guy feels wonderful. But while Mom is going back into the kitchen to rinse the glass, he gets back on his Big Wheel and cruises right into the street where he was told never to ride. Mom looks back out the living room window just as a Chevy screeches to a stop and then carefully eases its way around her precious son. She flies out the door, rushes into the street and picks up the boy, Big Wheel and all. As soon as they are back in the safety of their own yard, she starts yelling at him and spanking him.

The child wonders what is wrong with Mom. He suspects schizophrenia, but he doesn't want to say anything. His reaction is not the point, however—his life is at stake. Mom's behavior is saying, "That happy time five minutes ago with the lemonade and the hugs is a distant memory right now, because we are dealing with life and death. Your well-being is far more important than warm fuzzies."

One of the best definitions of tough love I know is *action for the well-being of the beloved.* We need more people who love others with such devotion that they will risk their current comfort level in the relationship and say whatever needs to be said in order to protect the other person's well-being.

"I love you so much that I can't stand by silently while you work yourself to death."

"I love you so much that I'm not going to pretend to be happy while you ruin your body by eating wrong, never exercising, drinking too much or smoking."

"I love you so much that I have to warn you you're not going to find what you're looking for in bars."

"I love you so much that I'm going to have to say you can't stay in this position in my firm any longer. It seems to be destroying you as a person, and I can't let that happen."

I went to a close friend one time when I saw his life taking a bad turn. I took him to a restaurant and said, "I'm not trying to run your life, but I'm concerned about the direction it's taking." He was so angry that he came close to leaping over the table to punch my lights out. So, man of valor that I am, I looked him in the eye and said, "Sorry, I'll never mention this again." I didn't, either, and he shipwrecked his life. I still see this friend occasionally, and many times I've said to him, "I failed you. I should have been on you like a shirt. I should have said, 'Leap over that table and deck me, if it will make you feel any better, but I'm going to tell you again that I'm concerned about your future.'" Maybe God would have used me if I had been a little more tenacious.

Whenever you take action on behalf of another person's well-being, you are taking a big risk. The comfort level between you may drop precipitously. Over time, however, the outcome of speaking the truth in love—especially when the relationship is basically mature and healthy—is usually positive. The obstacle in your relationship turns into a building block, and the two of you reach new understandings, make new commitments and establish deeper trust. But we all know that it is much easier to write and read about tough love than actually to sit down and have a heart-to-heart talk with someone. Confronting people can be frightening.

## Beware the Banana Room

My dad owned a produce company in Kalamazoo, Michigan. We had a large payroll: tough dockworkers, hard-drinking truck drivers, smooth salespeople and efficient managers. As could be expected with such an assortment of people, we had our share of relational problems.

I don't know how it all began, but even when I was a little boy I noticed that, whenever a problem had to be worked out between two employees, they would go into the banana room. Sometimes my dad or one of the other owners would say to someone, "I need to see you in the banana room." Sometimes a foreman would grab a dockworker and they would disappear in there.

The banana room was a temperature-controlled room containing up to 800 cases of bananas. It was completely enclosed and had a four-inch steel door, so no one outside could hear what was going on inside. Maybe that is why, when a summons to the banana room came, everybody quaked. "Oh no—not the banana room!" No one ever died in the banana room, and a lot of times after a discussion in there, people would come out smiling with their arms around each other. Still, people feared the banana room. They were terrified of the face-to-face, heart-to-heart discussions that always accompanied trips there.

Most of us prefer to avoid confrontation. We have a strong aversion to the very vehicle God has appointed to restore true peace between people! In Matthew 18:15, Jesus says, "If your brother sins against you, go and tell him his fault, between you and him alone. If he listens to you, you have gained your brother." Don't shove your feelings into a closet. Don't internalize your frustration. Instead, be tough. Schedule a heart-to-heart talk, and try to work out your differences.

## Prepare to Be Tough

But before making an appointment to get tough with somebody, it is important to prepare yourself. First of all, *clarify the issue.* What exactly is causing the tension in your relationship? Is it a mountain or a molehill? Is the problem temporary or lasting? Is the difficulty avoidable or unavoidable? Take out a pencil and paper and write down what you think is the root cause of the conflict you feel in this relationship.

Second, *cleanse your spirit.* Jesus said in Matthew 7:3-5: "Why do you see the speck that is in your brother's eye, but do not notice the log that is in your own eye? Or how can you say to your brother, 'Let me take the speck out of your eye,' when there is the log in your own eye? You hypocrite, first take the log out of your own eye, and then you will see clearly to take the speck out of your brother's eye." In other words, if you feel critical, angry and judgmental—if you can hardly wait to go in and wreak havoc—be careful. A heart-to-heart talk conducted with that attitude will not restore peace. Before calling your friend, surrender your spirit before God. Say, "God, I'm not ready yet. I'm too charged up. I have to cool off and get things in perspective. I need your Holy Spirit so I don't hurt somebody."

Third, *carefully select a time and place for your meeting.* For example the wife of a football fanatic should not plan on meaningful dialog during half time of the Super Bowl. Likewise, a husband should not expect his wife to listen eagerly while she is fixing dinner, the baby is crying and the two older children are fighting to the death in the next room. Plan to meet when you are both physically fresh, when you won't be hurried and where you can enjoy privacy.

Fourth, *pray.* God does amazing things when we ask him.

## Tough Does Not Mean Insensitive

When you prepare properly for a confrontation, you have won half the battle. You win the other half when you conduct the heart-to-heart talk sensitively. Here are three steps that will help you present your concerns clearly. They won't guarantee heartfelt thanks and warm fuzzies all around, but they will give you the best possible chance of being listened to and respected.

First, *begin with a sincere statement of commitment to the relationship.* If you're talking to your spouse, tell him or her that your marriage is the most important relationship in the world to you and that you want it to get even better. If you're talking to a friend, tell him or her how much you appreciate the friendship. If you're in a work situation, tell your supervisor that you enjoy working for her, or your employee that you're glad he's on your team. In all cases let the person you're talking to know that you're not issuing ultimatums—you're just trying to work on a problem.

Second, *make a careful, nonaccusatory explanation of the issue as you see it.* Avoid saying "you always" or "you never." When you say, "You're never home, Frank," Frank will answer, "You're wrong. I was home two years ago on February 4. You have blown this all out of proportion." But if you say, "I feel alone so much, Frank. I feel neglected. I feel frustrated and confused," Frank is more likely to listen. You may be crazy for having certain feelings, but he can hardly deny that you're having them. State the problem as carefully as you know how, using "I feel" statements whenever possible.

Third, *invite dialog.* After you have spilled your heart on the matter, ask, "Am I out to lunch on this? Do I have my facts straight? Am I missing something? Am I overly sensitive?" As a pastor, I am frequently challenged and confronted. When I sense in the challenger an open invitation to discuss the point, usually something can be worked out. But if someone finishes off an accusation by saying, in effect, "So there—I will allow you one phone call before I sentence you to an untimely death," I feel defensive. It is hard to reconcile with a person who has an attitude like that.

## The Results of Tough Love

Knowing the value of tough love, you have carefully prepared for a heart-to-heart confrontation, and you have conducted it with wisdom and restraint. What possible outcomes can you expect?

I wish I could guarantee that the person you love will say, "Thank you very much for bringing this to my attention." But it is not likely. You might get a slammed door, a pink slip or an earful of angry words. You might end up in big trouble. But if your relationship is built on deception, you are in big trouble already. So take the risk, make some waves and see what God does.

Most probably, the person will eventually take your words seriously, and your relationship will once again stand on firm ground. It is hard to resist someone who is humble and vulnerable. This may not happen immediately, however. Sometimes it takes several confrontations before the process is complete, and sometimes a relationship gets worse before it gets better. Some people excuse continuing hostilities by saying, "Well, I tried to patch it up once, and the other person wouldn't listen." But if your relationship has been disintegrating over months or years, reconciliation may take many attempts. It is unrealistic to expect one hour to undo the work of ten years.

Unfortunately, despite your best efforts, sometimes the person refuses to listen and your relationship seems to be worse off than before. In that case, try mediation. Bring in someone you both trust and respect, and let this person help you communicate. Your church may be able to help you find a mediator—the pastor, perhaps, or members who have dedicated themselves to this task, or maybe a small-group leader or elder. Or you may wish to discuss your problems with a professional counselor. I especially recommend this when alcohol or drug abuse is involved. Mediation may bring good results you cannot obtain on your own.

But we might as well face the facts—in some cases, tough love brings on permanent division. Paul says, "If possible, so far as it depends upon you, live peaceably with all" (Rom 12:18). But sometimes it isn't possible. For whatever reasons, sometimes the two of you will separate and go your own ways. When relationships are terminated, it breaks God's heart. But sometimes that is life in this sinful world; when it happens, we confess our sins, pick ourselves up and, by God's grace and with the help of our friends, we go on.

Too many of us, however, give up without a fight when a relationship begins to disintegrate. We scrap and claw and even go to court to protect our property, but all we do is cry a little when relationships die. This is backward thinking. Relationships are worth fighting for. Love needs to be tough enough to hang on.

Jesus' love for us is the tenderest love we will ever know. He died to heal our sins and to give us eternal life with him. He guides us, protects us, comforts us and nourishes us with his Word. But Jesus' love is also the toughest love we will ever face. He knows our hearts and does not hesitate to tell us when he finds sin there. He insists on truth no matter how painful it may be. He loves us too much to allow us to continue unchecked down a path of self-destruction.

Real love is always both tender and tough. May God give us the sensitivity to know when to show each kind of love and the courage to do whatever love demands.

# 8

# *Sacrificial Love*

## Giving without
## Giving Out

**A lot of** strange things are said about love. It's a many-splendored thing, a flower, a rose, a free-floating feeling of benevolence and good will toward all people, a scintillating opportunity to meet someone's need that will result in miraculous bonds of mutuality. In the contemporary view of love, what is important is not what I give to a relationship but what I get from it.

In today's view of love, the parable of the good Samaritan does not sound much like a love story. With a few modifications, however, it has real possibilities. Change the wounded traveler into a curvaceous blonde standing helplessly by her red Porsche, which has been incapacitated by a flat tire. In this retold story, you—the Samaritan—are able to change the tire without ever getting your hands or your three-piece suit dirty. The woman, of course, hovers nearby marveling at your skill and strength. Once the tire is changed and the tools put away, she hands you five crisp $100 bills, plants a wet kiss on your lips and says, "I don't know how I can thank you enough."

Somehow, though, love never works out that way for me. For some reason, real life more closely resembles the original parable. One January, for example, during a twenty-degree-below-zero Arctic blast, I was driving home from my workout at the gym when I noticed a middle-aged woman in a dirty Toyota pulled off the road in a snowbank. I fully intended to pass her by. I had things to do, people to see and places to go; not to mention wet hair, deck shoes, and no hat and gloves. But I felt the convicting voice of the Holy Spirit saying "Love," and I reluctantly turned around and went back.

The woman's trunk was full of books and clothes, and I had trouble finding the jack. When I finally found it, I was baffled about how to work it. Once I figured it out, my freezing hands stuck to it. And by the time I got the car off the ground, I discovered that there was no lug wrench in the trunk. Fortunately, the woman had a friend who lived only three blocks away. We were able to drive that far, and while she went in for hot chocolate, I stayed out in the unheated garage and finished the job. She thanked me and drove away, and I dragged my frostbitten body into my car and drove home, saying to myself as my brain thawed out, "Where is this many-splendored thing they sing about? If I ever find it, I'll kill it."

## Love Is Sacrifice

I have found that love is a lot more closely related to work than to play. It has a lot more to do with being a servant than with being a hero. When I set about the task of loving, I usually end up giving instead of receiving. Love inevitably costs me something, usually the three commodities most precious to me—my time, my energy and my money. I do not easily part with these resources, because I have them in limited quantities.

Tell me how to show love without spending time, energy or money and I will gladly sign up. Tell me that love means sacrifice, however, and I become reluctant to commit myself. Maybe that is why some Christians emphasize the fun, fellowship and fulfillment aspects of Christianity without ever mentioning the sacrifice. It is high time to strip away the false glamour that the world—and sometimes the church—puts on loving. It's time to tell the truth: *true love is sacrificial.*

The most famous verse in the Bible, John 3:16, gives the biblical definition of love: "God so loved the world that he gave his only Son, that whoever believes in him should not perish but have eternal life." Because God was concerned with the well-being of people who were precious to him, he *gave*—he sacrificed—his only Son; and when you are concerned about the well-being of others, you usually have to sacrifice too. You may have to expend your time, your energy or your money for them. You may have to give up your plans, your independence or your privacy. To love as God loves, you may have to part with whatever is most precious to you for the sake of other people.

Sacrificial love is a difficult concept to grasp, because our culture teaches the exact opposite. We are constantly bombarded with books, articles, radio and TV shows, commercials and ads shouting, "You are number one. Take care of yourself. Don't let others steal your time. Save your energy so you can enjoy leisure moments. Stockpile financial resources so you can spend more on yourself. If you protect your time, conserve your energy, and amass your resources, you will be happy."

I did not realize how much I had bought into today's misplaced values until, during my junior year in college, I was shocked awake by a professor's statement: "True personal fulfillment never comes through self-gratification."

"That is the boldest, most radical, most countercultural statement I have ever heard," I thought. "It flies in the face of everything I've been taught." But, I began to realize, it does not fly in the face of Jesus' teachings. "If any man would come after me," Jesus said, "let him deny himself and take up his cross and follow me. For whoever would save his life will lose it; and whoever loses his life for my sake and the gospel's will save it" (Mk 8:34-35). "Whoever would be great among you must be your servant . . . for the Son of man also came not to be served but to serve, and to give his life as a ransom for many" (Mk 10:43-45).

The world writes books with titles like *Think and Grow Rich*. If Jesus were writing for today's market, he might call his book *Love and Give Everything Away*. Paradoxically, when you give yourself to God and serve his people in sacrificial love, you find a fulfillment and satisfaction the world never experiences.

## Sacrificial Love in Marriage

Let's get specific. How does sacrificial love operate in marriage?

According to the world's wisdom, a good marriage enhances the life of each spouse, making it fuller and more satisfying than it would be if the marriage did not exist. Marriage, then, should not inhibit either spouse from living up to his or her full potential. One spouse should not put the other's needs above his or her own; this will lead to loss of personhood. In a marriage like this, if either spouse discovers he or she is giving more than he or she is getting, a power struggle is likely to ensue. If reciprocal rights cannot be agreed on and guaranteed, the marriage is often dissolved.

The world's view of marriage emphasizes maximum pleasure with minimum sacrifice. It does not take into account possibilities such as incapacitating illness, emotional disturbance, financial reversals or even the arrival of a helpless but demanding baby. That is why this view of marriage is not working, why the divorce rate has soared almost beyond comprehension. Love has never been able to operate for long without sacrifice.

God's wisdom is completely different from the world's. In a biblical marriage, each partner looks the other in the eye and says, "I love you, which by definition means I commit myself to serve you, to build you up, to cheer you on. I know full well this is going to cost me lots of time, energy and money, but I want to put your interests ahead of mine. I'll stand at the back of the line; you go first."

In a biblical marriage, there is no power struggle with each partner trying to gain the upper hand. Instead, there is a serving contest in which each is trying to outlove, outbless and outserve the other. My wife knows how to love sacrificially. One night recently I took her out to dinner, and she said to me, "I've been noticing that the demands on your life are increasing. Maybe I should quit writing and concentrate on making your life smoother."

Although I was tempted to say, "Great! And while you're at it, will you give me a backrub?" I held back, because I knew she was offering me one of her dearest treasures. "No," I said, "I really want you to develop your potential. Don't quit writing. Maybe I should say no to more things so you can continue to grow and flourish." And right there in the restaurant, we got into an argument—not the kind that destroys, but the kind that builds up.

Sacrificial love is the backbone of lasting marriages, even when it leads to impasses in restaurants. It is also the backbone of strong friendships.

## Expending Yourself for Your Friends

The world does not understand the Christian concept of brotherhood and sisterhood. The world says to find friends among like-minded, like-incomed people who vote like you and have about the same golf handicap. These are safe people; they won't start asking for counseling or financial assistance. If you keep a healthy distance from them, the relationship won't get muddied up with commitments or expectations.

These friendships work until the bottom falls out of your life. You face a pressing problem, a tragic loss or a serious illness, and suddenly you realize that no one cares much about you. You made no investment in anybody else's life, and so now when you need to make a withdrawal, there's no money in the friendship bank.

Christian friendship is different. You find a few brothers and sisters and decide at the outset that you are going to expend yourself for them. You invest time, energy and often money in them. Because you meet regularly and talk, you get into each other's lives. You encourage, counsel, challenge and rebuke each other. You make sacrifices. Some time ago, a close brother wrote me a letter that began, "This letter is in part to tell you formally that whatever I have is yours. If you and your family ever need any kind of help, just say the word." A colleague once told me, "I know I could go to the phone right now and call five friends who would give me a car, a hand, a place to live if I needed it. This is one of the greatest blessings of my life."

Such sacrificial love is the foundation of true friendships and strong marriages. It also has many other applications. In the business world, for example, it can change the way we treat our colleagues, employees and customers. In our communities, it can reach out to many people and make their lives better.

My father always ended his letters to me with the phrase, "Love those people who need love the most." He put his words into practice in Kalamazoo, Michigan, where he helped a blind man start a restaurant, worked on providing safe shelter for vagrants in the downtown area and, when Vietnamese refugees flooded the country, adopted four or five families and found housing, cars and jobs for them. In addition to his heavy work responsibilities, every week for twenty-five years on Sunday afternoons my father led a hymn sing and Bible study for a hundred mentally retarded women at the state hospital. That is sacrificial love, and today's world desperately needs more of it.

## Burnout!

Sacrificial love has just one problem. If you really commit yourself to it, you will quickly find out that it is extremely exhausting. After a certain amount of giving and serving and expending, you may begin to feel numb, as if you have nothing left to give. You are running on empty.

Some people with strong moral fiber and good self-discipline say, "Even though I'm all out of love, I'm going to keep on giving. It's the action that matters, not the feelings." Although they are entirely right about that, they still eventually come to the point of being not only empty, but angry. Angry at people who matter to God, maybe even angry at God himself.

People become problems to be avoided. Phone calls become intrusions. Letters, even from friends, are simply obligations to attend to. Unexpected guests are invaders. Everyone who is on the front lines of loving others knows the feeling: "I can't handle another heartache, another need, another hurt—another person. I want to run away, build a wall around myself, and become a hermit." At that point the great temptation arises to give up altogether on loving people. I frequently hear people say, "I used to be actively involved with others. I used to have relationships and be in ministries. But I burned out, and now I stay away from commitments to people." That is one way of handling burnout, of course. But there is a better way.

It is possible to run completely out of love and then refill the tank. It is possible to love people not only sacrificially but also steadfastly. This is what God calls us to do—not to run the hundred-yard dash in loving people but to run the marathon. In order to do that, we have to learn how to refuel ourselves when we run out of love.

## Spiritual Refueling

In 1 Samuel 30 we find a little-known episode in David's life before he becomes king, while he is still an outlawed rebel leader. David has been loving and leading and helping and serving people until he is nearly out of love. His tank is almost dry when an opposition force ambushes the camp and carries off the wives and children of David and his men. The men, outraged, talk of overthrowing David and even killing him. David can't take any more. He feels like pitching his leadership position. He would like to spit on the ground and leave the people. He's sick of them, and he's exhausted. What can he do?

The answer is found in an amazing little phrase, "David encouraged himself in the LORD his God" (v. 6 KJV). He left the people with their incessant demands. He turned his back on still more opportunities for service. He took time out, got away by himself and had a long talk with God. For a little while he basked in God's love for him. He remembered that "God is our refuge and strength, a very present help in trouble" (Ps 46:1). He spent time in solitude with God until his spiritual energy supply was replenished.

Jesus did the same thing after long periods of loving, serving, healing, counseling and teaching. "After he had dismissed the crowds, he went up on the mountain by himself to pray" (Mt 14:23). "Great multitudes gathered to hear and to be healed of their infirmities. But he withdrew to the wilderness and prayed" (Lk 5:15-16). He needed time alone with the Father to replenish himself. It goes without saying that, if David and Jesus needed spiritual refueling from time to time, so do we.

Somehow we must learn to slow down, get off the treadmill,

seek out solitude and encourage ourselves in God. One way to do this is through a daily time of solitude, perhaps before the events of the day rush in. Talk with the Lord and read his Word. Allow him to regenerate your spiritual energies. Some people find spiritual refueling by listening to Christian music tapes. Sometimes when I'm driving to an appointment, feeling stretched to the limit, I turn off the news with its catastrophes and commercials and put in a worship tape. After a half-hour on the road, my spirit is refreshed by the Spirit of the Lord.

I know a man who takes fifteen minutes of his lunch hour to spiritually refuel. Almost every day he closes his office door and reads promises from God's Word. Other people take walks every night, worshiping God as they walk, while still others play musical instruments, read Christian books or sing choruses to the Lord. There's no one right way to encourage yourself in the Lord; the possibilities are endless. Experiment until you find a way that's right for you, because when you learn to do this, you will be well on your way toward loving sacrificially and steadfastly.

## Emotional Refueling

It is important to watch your spiritual fuel gauge, though that is not the only indicator that may register empty. You also have to watch your emotional fuel gauge as well. It is possible to keep your spiritual reserves replenished and still feel all out of love.

Major life changes can drain you emotionally: the death of a spouse, divorce, personal injury or illness, loss of employment, change of residence. Even happy events, such as family holidays or the birth of a child, can leave you emotionally spent.

A friend of mine recently had five extremely difficult conversations in one day. When he left the office that evening, he was doing great spiritually—but he was emotionally depleted. Similar experiences happen often in the marketplace. You must fire somebody or reorganize something. Your supervisor makes you redo a major project. The computer goes down for the day. Emotional depletion also happens at home. The sink backs up and the plumber is busy until the end of the week. Chicken pox attacks the children one by one. You learn that your teen-aged son has a drug problem. When your emotional tank is empty, you are likely to feel uninterested in the well-being of others, no matter how full your spiritual tank is.

How do you replenish yourself emotionally? There are basically two ways. First, *relaxation.* Some people cannot accept that. They like the fast track, and if they need emotional refueling, they prefer to get it from a pill or an injection. But there is no quick solution. To fill up your emotional reserves, you need to wind down, take a break, put your feet up, take deep breaths and hold the phone calls. Let nature take its course and restore you to your usual emotional strength.

The second way to replenish yourself emotionally is *recreation.* Some activities seem to inspire you, to re-create your enthusiasm for life. For my wife, it's reading, writing and playing the flute. For me, it's sailing. For you it may be walking the dog, playing racquetball or weeding the garden. You may have to experiment for a while to find what works best for you. When you find it, you'll know. A couple of hours of the activity, whatever it is, will refuel you emotionally and make it possible for you to go back to loving others sacrificially and steadfastly.

## Physical Refueling

If your spiritual and emotional reserves are full and you still feel like hiding under your desk whenever you hear footsteps in the hall, you may need to check your physical fuel gauge.

One Wednesday night before Thanksgiving, I went to a rather lengthy meeting at church before driving with my family to Michigan. Although we did not get to bed there until five in the morning, we had to get up early and start visiting with the relatives. I was in fine shape spiritually that Thanksgiving morning and in reasonable shape emotionally. But physically I was shot.

Every conversation was like hard labor for me. Someone would tell a joke and I would think, "Don't be a jerk, Bill—laugh!" Relatives came to me, hoping for some input about a major decision they were making. But as I talked with them a little voice in my head was saying, "Why don't you handle your own problems? I didn't come here to do counseling. I came for turkey and football. If you want an appointment, call my secretary. I'm sure there's an opening in June." I tried hard to hide how I really felt, and I doubt that any major family damage occurred. But not until late Friday, after I had had time to recuperate physically, did I feel like myself again.

A lot of people these days are chronically run down physically. Most have no idea how much their physical condition undermines their attempts to love other people. They fail to realize that it takes physical energy to listen, to serve, to confront, to rebuke. Not only are physically run-down people short on energy; they also tend to be easily irritated, critical, short fused, defensive and negative. It is hard for them to love others and it is equally hard for others to love them.

How do you stay physically fit? You know the three rules. Eat right, sleep enough, and exercise. Most Americans eat far too much sugar and fat; consequently, many of us are overweight. It is also why we suffer from sugar highs and sugar lows, and it has a lot to do with our high rate of heart disease. It is impossible to maintain good physical reserves on a junk-food diet.

In addition, many of us are careless about sleep. If you do not wake up reasonably refreshed, maybe you are not spending enough time in bed. Or maybe the time you spend there is less than refreshing because the coffee you drank all day or the pepperoni pizza you ate at midnight is keeping you awake.

And for far too many of us, our major form of exercise is

walking down the hall to the photocopy machine. We say we don't have time or energy to exercise, yet experts have medically proven that exercise replenishes the energy supply and actually decreases the need for sleep.

If you are spiritually and emotionally on track, but still feel burned out, check your diet, your sleep and your exercise. A few simple changes in your daily habits might be just what you need to refuel your tank and refit you for steadfast, sacrificial loving.

## The Rewards of Sacrifice

Real loving is not easy. It will cost you more than you can imagine. After you have spent all the time, energy and money that you can spare, you will have to take time out for refueling in order to keep on spending your resources. But sacrificial loving will reward you more than you ever dreamed.

The Bible tells about a time when Peter began to wonder if all his sacrifices were worth it. "Then Peter said . . . 'Lo, we have left everything and followed you. What then shall we have?' Jesus said to them, 'Truly, I say to you, in the new world, when the Son of man shall sit on his glorious throne, you who have followed me will also sit on twelve thrones, judging the twelve tribes of Israel. And every one who has left houses or brothers or sisters or father or mother or children or lands, for my name's sake, will receive a hundredfold, and inherit eternal life' " (Mt 19:27-29).

If you give yourself to God and to others, God will register your sacrifice in heaven's ledger sheets. He will pour out a return so bountiful that, over a period of time, you will marvel at how full your life is. You will find yourself breaking out in spontaneous bursts of worship. You will hear yourself singing, "You satisfy my soul. You give me life in all its fullness." Today's imitation love offers no such rewards. As my professor said, "True personal fulfillment never comes through self-gratification." Instead, it comes through sacrifice.

# 9

# *Radical Love*

## Breaking the
## Hostility Cycle

**We have looked** at love from several angles. We have seen that it needs to be tough as well as tender, and it almost always requires us to sacrifice. Jesus shows us yet another angle on love in Matthew 5:39-41, part of the Sermon on the Mount: "I say to you, Do not resist one who is evil. But if any one strikes you on the right cheek, turn to him the other also; and if any one would sue you and take your coat, let him have your cloak as well; and if any one forces you to go one mile, go with him two miles."

I think that when Jesus preached these now-familiar words, he was trying to startle his disciples into taking the next step in their understanding of Christian love. He was saying to them, "Fellas, you are making reasonable progress in understanding what it means to follow me, but when it comes to understanding the kind of interpersonal relationships I want you to have, you need some straightforward, practical, eye-opening information. So listen closely to a few down-to-earth, everyday illustrations about what it means to love as I love."

## A Slap in the Face

Consider how Jesus' illustrations must have sounded to the disciples:

Picture yourself walking through the busy streets of Jerusalem. You happen to notice some men standing on a corner discussing politics. You know a few of them and so you amble over and begin to listen to what they're saying. Then someone asks you to explain your views on the Jerusalem political scene. You enthusiastically comply, offering a few well-thought-out suggestions that would solve Jerusalem's problems, knowing full well that some of them are rather bold. Out of the corner of your eye you notice that one of the men is getting red-faced with anger. All of a sudden he squares off in front of you and, with all the pomp his indignation can muster, gives you a backhanded slap across the face.

In the culture of first-century Jerusalem, receiving a slap in the face was considered the ultimate degradation. Even today when we are insulted we say, "That was a real slap in the face." There's no doubt about it—you have been publicly humiliated by an arrogant, opinionated ignoramus. You can still feel the sting of his slap on your face. Your adrenaline is flowing; your anger level is skyrocketing. Your *honor* is at stake. You know you could knock this guy into the middle of next week if you wanted to. And inside your head, voices are saying, "Rocky, Rocky, Rocky . . ."

The moment of truth has arrived. What are you going to do? In the Sermon on the Mount, Jesus commands his followers to show *radical love*. Don't slap him back. Don't scream at him. Don't kick him in the shins. Don't curse him under your breath. Instead, look the man straight in the eye and remind yourself that, in spite of his arrogance and anger, he matters to God. Even at that moment God is trying to reach out to him. In fact, he is looking for someone through whom he could love this guy. So dig down deep into the foundations of your faith and love him. Do something radical that will mark his life. If turning the other cheek to him for a second slap will make a mark on the man's soul, turn the other cheek.

Can you imagine how hard it must have been for the disciples to hear Jesus' challenge? Born and raised in a revenge-oriented culture, they knew all about male honor, bravado and machismo. Turn the other cheek? What a crazy idea!

## Beyond Legal Rights

Jesus' second illustration requires a brief explanation of the Middle Eastern wardrobe in New Testament times. People wore an inner garment of a soft fabric next to the skin. Most people had several sets of these. Over the inner garment they wore a heavy, warm, loose-fitting outer garment that served a dual purpose. During the day it was like a suit coat or sport jacket, but at night it functioned as a blanket.

In that climate a man without an outer garment for warmth at night was in a bad way. So important was the outer garment, in fact, that it was protected by law. During trading and bartering sessions, it was common for men to hold each other's garments as collateral until the deal was consummated and the good delivered. Usually the inner garment was demanded, because even a poor man would have an extra one. Ordinarily the outer garment was not used, because it was illegal to keep another man's outer garment overnight, even if the man reneged on his part of the deal. The cloak had to be returned at sunset, because without it he would have nothing to protect him from the night's chill.

In view of the importance of the outer garment, Jesus' command is amazing. If you are making a deal with someone and for some reason can't come through with your end of it, and if that man demands an inner garment as overnight collateral, give it to him, of course. But go a step further. Offer him your outer garment as well. Look him in the eye and say, "I know what's right. A deal is a deal, and I have not fulfilled my part. So please take my outer garment, even though by law I am entitled to keep it. It is important to me to be known as a trustworthy trader, and I can get by for a night without my cloak. And, by the way, is there any other service I can render to your family?"

According to Jesus, the demands of radical love often exceed those of any written law. Love never seeks to get away with doing the bare minimum. It goes beyond law keeping and offers outrageous service.

## The Second Mile

This leads to Jesus' third illustration, one that cuts to the very souls of his listeners because it had to do with a practice they all absolutely detested—*impressment*. In those days Israel was ruled by Rome. Governors were stationed throughout the empire, and soldiers occupied the various provinces. A Roman soldier had the legal right to approach any civilian at any time of the day or night and impress—that is, coerce—him into service. The soldier could force the civilian to make meals, do laundry, provide lodging or whatever else the soldier thought needed to be done.

The Jews particularly hated it when a Roman soldier made them carry baggage. Whenever troop assignments were shifted, soldiers would appear, tap Jewish men on the shoulder with spears, and say, "Carry that suitcase and that duffel bag, and do it quickly." No matter what the civilian was doing—sleeping, plowing a field, selling his wares—he would have to quit and do as the soldier said. There was a limit, however. The Jews hated this practice so intensely that apparently the Roman officers instructed their men to restrict their demands. They could force a Jewish man to carry baggage for no more than a mile at a time.

So suppose a Roman soldier grabs you by the scruff of the neck, pushes a heavy suitcase into your stomach and says, "Carry this, pal." He walks leisurely along beside you, eating grapes, while you stumble and strain to carry his suitcase. How does Jesus say to respond? When you get to the end of the obligatory mile, instead of slamming the suitcase to the ground hoping to break something fragile inside, instead of shaking the dust off your robe and spitting on the ground to show your contempt for this pagan soldier and this detestable practice, show him radical love.

When you get to the end of that mile, say, "Sir, could I be of further service to you in any way? God has put love in my heart for all his creations, and that includes you, whether you are aware of it or not. You matter so much to him that it would be a privilege for me to be able to serve you. So if you want to go another mile together, I'll go with you."

## Understanding the Stories
As Jesus clearly taught, the highest priority in the life of every believer should be to love God with all our hearts, souls and minds (Mt 22:37-40). Our second-highest priority should be to love people, all of whom matter to God, in a radical, nonretaliatory, second-mile way.

For two thousand years people have read and reread Jesus' Sermon on the Mount, asking the Spirit of God to help them understand and apply these three illustrations. Believers have drawn a wide range of conclusions from them, and I still have a lot of questions about their implications myself. But these stories have some general applications that are as plain as can be. There's no mystery about them.

One obvious principle taught by these stories is that retaliation is a dead-end road. Revenge only perpetrates and escalates animosity. Somebody has to stop the senseless escalation—and God wants that someone to be me.

Another clear implication of these stories is that male honor is not the most important thing in the world. I have to learn how to absorb some everyday slaps—being cut off in traffic, having someone push in line in front of me or being interrupted in a conversation. I need to become less defensive, and learn how to absorb some shots instead of returning them.

Finally, the stories plainly point out the secret power of the second mile. When we exceed the barest minimums of service, when we go beyond the call of duty, it has an effect on people that they do not soon forget.

Jesus' way of loving was radically new. Old Testament laws carefully preserved justice—"an eye for an eye and a tooth for a tooth"—but Jesus went far beyond justice in these three illustrations. Why did he want his disciples to be radical, nonretaliatory, second-mile lovers?

## Breaking the Vicious Circle

First, God knows it takes a radical lover to break the cycle of interpersonal hostility. The day "Cain rose up against his brother Abel, and killed him" (Gen 4:8), this cycle was set in motion, and it has continued unabated ever since.

A friend of mine is a paramedic in Humboldt Park, a Chicago neighborhood notorious for its gangs. "You know how it goes," he told me. "It starts with a little misunderstanding. It escalates when someone gets his feelings hurt and uses a little sarcastic language. His sarcasm provokes a smart-aleck response, which elicits a threat and then a challenge. Now the male bravado and honor get going. And then come the fists and the clubs and the knives and the guns. The blood flows and the flesh tears, and when it's all over and people are lying in piles, they call us and we come in and pick up the pieces."

I know how it goes. It's been going that way for thousands of years. Granted, in a "sophisticated suburban" environment most of our hostilities do not end in hand-to-hand combat. They end in cold wars: detachment, distrust, alienation, bitterness, name calling, mudslinging, separation, isolation and lawsuits. Although we rarely fight with our fists, we can do a great deal of damage without ever soiling our three-piece suits.

But the cycle of hostility must be stopped if there is ever going to be relational harmony in this world, and it will take radical, nonretaliatory, second-mile lovers to stop it. Somebody has to take a blow, insult or slap instead of returning it. Somebody has to absorb an injustice instead of inflicting another one on somebody else; somebody has to pull the plug on continued cruelty. God says, "You can do it, if you're willing to become a radical lover."

In your marriage, are you willing to be the one to break the icy silences when feelings have been hurt? In the workplace, are you willing to say, "I apologize—let me help with one of your projects so your load will be easier"? In school, are you willing to complete your assignments cheerfully and then offer to do more, even—especially—if the teacher or professor is unpleasant and demanding? God is looking for radical lovers who will report for duty.

## Radical Love As Evangelism

The second reason why God challenges us to become radical, nonretaliatory, second-mile lovers is that nothing leaves a deeper mark on the lives of spiritually hardened men and women than seeing radical love in action. If you know the love of Jesus Christ in a personal way, you may sometimes lie awake nights thinking of ways to make a mark on people's lives so that they too will come to enjoy what you have found. Should you wear a little lapel pin? Put a bumper sticker on your car? Display a large Bible in your office? Tell people that you don't go to movies or buy sexually explicit rock albums? Jesus says, if you really want to make a deep, lasting mark on someone, demonstrate radical love. There is so much compelling power in that kind of love that it makes callous people's heads spin. They cannot figure out why you are giving up your rights and letting someone take advantage of you.

Jesus showed radical love all his life. At the end he took slaps without saying anything. He absorbed beatings without cursing anyone. When nails were pounded into his hands and feet, he did not turn to the people doing the pounding and say, "You're going to rot in hell for this!" No, he said, "Father, these men matter to you. Don't charge this crime to their account. Forgive them, if that's possible."

As Jesus died, a Clint Eastwood kind of man, a hardened Roman officer, broke down and cried, "Surely this was the Son of God!" I doubt if the army man had ever heard any theology, but he was broken by the power of Jesus' radical, nonretaliatory, second-mile love.

## A Gateway into Christ's Presence

A third reason God asks us to show this kind of love is that it knits the soul of the radical lover to the heart of God.

I know a man who has an unusual rapport with God. He was not born that way; he drew close to God through practicing radical love. Some years ago, he and his father were missionaries in a faraway land. Representatives of another religious sect asked the father if they might pray with him. He readily agreed, and a date was set. When the time came, a man arrived, and the two of them went into a private room to pray. Suddenly my friend heard a great deal of commotion. Rushing into the room, he discovered his father bleeding on the floor. The visiting man, instead of praying with him, had stabbed him to death.

The younger man, in spite of his grief, decided to dedicate himself to reaching the very religious sect that had arranged for his father's murder. No one would have blamed him for leaving the ministry. But rather than leaving, he actually expanded the work his father had begun—and in the process of radically loving his father's killers, he learned to feel Christ's presence and power as he had never felt them before.

When you take slaps, give up your legal rights and carry baggage a lot farther than you need to, you find yourself out in deep water with Christ. Realizing that the ground is not solid beneath your feet, you cling to him. You feel his support in ways you would normally never notice. Most people never leave the harbors of love. They are afraid to venture out on the high seas of radical, nonretaliatory, second-mile love. But that's where the action is. That's where God's presence manifests itself in a far greater way than shorebound people could ever imagine. That is where people are startled into taking a closer look at Jesus Christ, the world's only perfect example of radical love. That is also where hostilities die and lasting peace begins.

Radical love does not make sense. It is not easy. But it is something that the world desperately needs, now more than ever.

# 10

## The

# *Character*

### of Christ

**A friend of** mine once asked me to teach a class of fifth-and sixth-grade campers. After a session with the children during which I gave them a simple message on how to receive Christ, a boy of about ten approached me and said, "You talked about asking Jesus into your heart. Before I do that, can you tell me what he's like?"

Realizing he was looking for a three-minute answer, not a seminary course, I opened my Bible and turned to John 10. This is what we read together: "The thief comes only to steal and kill and destroy; I came that they may have life, and have it abundantly. I am the good shepherd. The good shepherd lays down his life for the sheep. He who is a hireling and not a shepherd, whose own the sheep are not, sees the wolf coming and leaves the sheep and flees; and the wolf snatches them and scatters them. He flees because he is a hireling and cares nothing for the sheep. I am the good shepherd; I know my own and my own know me, as the Father knows me and I know the Father; and I lay down my life for the sheep" (vv. 10-15).

Jesus is a great teacher. Knowing that most people think in pictures, he gives a picture of himself as a good shepherd. Realizing that most people have misconceptions about why he wants to come into their lives, he begins revealing his character by telling who he is *not*.

## Not a Thief

"I am not like a thief," Jesus says. A burglar's basic aim is to break into your house and find something of great value that will get good money on the market. You hardly ever hear of a thief who makes off with four dishtowels, two throw rugs and a tube of toothpaste; thieves look for jewelry, family heirlooms, paintings and electronic equipment. That's the character of a thief—to find what is precious and steal it.

Jesus is the exact opposite of a thief. He does not come to rob but to give. He does not break into anyone's life; he stands at the door and knocks. If invited in, he wanders around the house placing precious objects on the mantels, on the shelves and in the cupboards. He fills up the person's life with everything life is worth living for: purpose, fulfillment, meaning, love, peace, confidence, security and even freedom.

A lot of people don't understand that about Jesus. They fear he wants to break into their lives and rob them of the joy of living. They are sure he wants to limit their freedom and make them live in confinement. They suspect he wants to take away fulfillment, put an end to adventure and stop the fun. Sometimes these people come to me and say, "I sense that God wants greater control of my life, and I don't want to let him in. I'm fighting him."

I usually tell them, "Don't worry—you'll win. You can keep God out. Slam the door, put bars on the windows and close your mind. You can stop him." But I also tell them that they don't understand who Jesus is. He is not a thief but an anti-thief. He knocks patiently until you open the door, and then he fills up your house with a whole truckload of life's most precious commodities.

Christ is an altruistic lover: he loves us for what he can give us, not for what he can get from us. If you tear down the bars on the windows, unbolt your doors and fling them wide open so that he can come in, he will fill your house with everything it needs in order to be warm, and beautiful and pleasant to live in.

## Two Kinds of Shepherds

Jesus, then, is a shepherd, not a thief. But there are two kinds of shepherds—owners and hired hands. A hireling makes a daily or hourly wage in exchange for doing what the owner asks. He tends to do whatever is necessary to earn his paycheck, but not a bit more. For a hireling, there is no emotion, no compassion, no fulfillment, no overtime and no extra mile.

While I was going to college, I was a hireling. I worked for a butcher, chopping up chickens. It was a job, but that was all. Sometimes the boss would say, "Bill, we're going to have a special sale tomorrow. Do you think you could stay a little later tonight?" I tried to answer politely, but inside I was thinking, "I don't care if this building burns down; I'm out of here at five o'clock." That's the attitude of a hireling.

An owner has a very different attitude. When my father's produce company had a load of vegetables that had to be halfway across the continent by a certain deadline, he sent my brother or me, not a hired driver, to deliver it. If there was a field that had to be plowed at exactly the right time for planting, he sent my brother or me, not hired field hands, to plow it. We were owners, and we cared!

Every day of the week I drive down a road lined with privately owned businesses. Monday through Friday the parking lots are always filled. On Saturday mornings, however, only one car is usually parked in front of each business— and it looks very much like the owner's car. Why? Because the business belongs to him. He probably built it up from nothing, and he wants to keep a close watch on the statistics, the cash flow, the deposits and the statements. He cares about it in a way his employees can never understand.

Jesus is a caring owner. We are his sheep, not someone else's, and he will walk miles to lead us to green pastures. He counts and recounts us. He protects us from impending danger, and he even laid down his life for our sakes. Because he owns us and loves us, Jesus monitors every step we take. He knows every hurt we feel, every crushing disappointment we experience. He is in love with us, and he will do whatever it takes to keep us safe in his flock.

## Sons and Daughters, Not Slaves

Because Jesus is our shepherd, we can become personal friends of his. "I know my own and my own know me," he said, "as the Father knows me and I know the Father" (Jn 10:14-15). In other words, the relationship between us and our shepherd can be as close as the relationship between Jesus and his heavenly Father— what a mind-stretching thought!

To help us understand the depth and permanence of such a relationship, Scripture uses another picture to describe it. In Romans 8:14-17, Paul writes, "All who are led by the Spirit of God are sons of God. For you did not receive the spirit of slavery to fall back into fear, but you have received the spirit of sonship ["adoption," KJV]. When we cry, 'Abba! Father!' it is the Spirit himself bearing witness with our spirit that we are children of God, and if children, then heirs, heirs of God and fellow heirs with Christ."

Jesus does not want us to relate to him out of fear, as a slave relates to a master. Over a century has passed since the Emancipation Proclamation, and we may not be able to feel the degradation of being a slave. Most of us have never belonged to a human master with total power over us, including the authority to injure us, kill us or break up our families. But we still have employers to relate to, and we still know what it means to be fearful.

A few years ago, on a plane bound for Los Angeles, I sat next to a person who worked for a well-known international conglomerate. This man said to me, "We do our work on a quota basis. If we come through with sales that meet or exceed the quotas, there's a future for us in the company. So far, for the eleven years I've been with the company, I've been able to do it. But they upped my quota last quarter, and I don't think I'm going to make it. That means my job is in jeopardy."

Eleven years of faithful work for the company and if he falls short of one quota, he's out! That employee could hardly miss the message—his value is tied to his performance; the performance must always improve and mistakes will not be tolerated. Jesus Christ says, "I want none of that. I don't want my people to be terrified slaves. I don't want them to think I love them because of what they can do for me. I want them to know I love them for who they are—the adopted sons and daughters of God, my brothers and sisters. And I don't want them to fear being thrown out on the street for whatever reason; I want them to know they are in my family forever."

## Our Adoptive Father

A few years ago, Lynne and I took in an eight-year-old boy and a three-year-old girl who, because of their parents' alcoholism and divorce, had been passed from home to home. For several months they lived with us, and we grew to love them. I had bought the boy a model car that he really enjoyed putting together. He had worked on it for two weeks and was just putting the finishing touches on it when I had to tell him that the next day the authorities were transferring him to another home. Tears came to his eyes, and then he got angry. He took his little fist and hit the model right on its top, shattering it into a million pieces. "I feel like a football," he said.

All human beings long for family permanence, but most of us quickly learn that it will not be found in an earthly family. A parent dies. A couple gets divorced. Grandparents move far away. Our families do not fill our yearning for a home and family that endures. Christ recognizes that need and meets us by adopting us into his family. He gives us his name: we are called Christians. He gives us his inheritance: life eternal.

I know couples with hearts full of love who yearn to focus that love toward some little one, but no little one arrives. When these couples find children to adopt, they are absolutely thrilled. They don't warn the children that they had better come up to expectations if they want to remain with them. They don't tell thim that they are allowed three mistakes, and then it's back to the agency. They accept them with open arms and joy-filled hearts because they love them, and they take them into their homes forever, give them the family name, and make them legal heirs. That is exactly how God acts when he adopts us into his family.

Just as a husband and wife who decide to give birth to or adopt a child begin to plan for that child long before it is born, God has arranged to take us into his family long before we realize our need for him. As Paul says in his letter to the Ephesians 1:4-5, "He chose us in him before the creation of the world to be holy and blameless in his sight. In love he predestined us to be adopted as his sons through Jesus Christ" (1:45 NIV).

God is saying to us, "My heart is so filled with love that I want to take you in and make you a permanent part of my family. Anybody—of any race, color, creed, background or hang-up—is welcome in my adoptive family." When we sincerely say, "Lord Jesus, I want to be a part of your family," the transaction is consummated and our adoption becomes legally binding and permanent. From then on, we no longer have the spirit of slavery. We are sons and daughters of God.

## Confidence in the Spirit

In today's culture we thrive on legal documents. When you get married, you get a marriage license. When you buy a home, you get a title. When you buy a car, you get registration papers. In a transaction as important as adoption into God's family, some form of evidence that the transaction has taken place is important, and the evidence God has given us is more important and more binding than any piece of paper—it is the daily and hourly announcement of the Holy Spirit to our own spirits that we belong to God.

God does not want us to wonder how we stand with him. That is why "the Spirit himself bear[s] witness with our spirit that we are children of God" (Rom 8:16). The inner witness of the Spirit is mysterious. I cannot explain it or always describe it, but I can testify that it is real. When people say to me, "I don't know if I'm a Christian or not. I think I might be. I hope I am," I get worried, because the Bible clearly states that when you give your heart to the Lord, he becomes real to you and you know you belong to him (see, for example, 2 Cor 1:22; Eph 1:13-14; 1 Jn 3:24; 4:13). The Holy Spirit lives inside you and repeatedly whispers, "Have confidence—you are part of God's family."

The Spirit's witness shows how Christ loves us—not as statistics in the heavenly census records, not as voices in the vast heavenly choir, but as individual, significant human beings. He does not want us to be timid or fearful, to live under the constant threat of condemnation. He wants us to be aware of the gift he has given us and secure in his love. He loves us as a brother would love us, because that is exactly who he is.

## Fellow Heirs with Christ

Some people think of the Fatherhood of God and our adoption into Christ's family as a lovely metaphor, a divinely inspired figure of speech that helps us understand the depths of God's love for us. This is true, but it does not go far enough. God has *literally* taken us into his family: the proof is that he offers us a share in the estate. If we are children, says Paul, we are heirs—"fellow heirs with Christ" (Rom 8:17). Along with Christ, God's beloved Son, we will receive part of the inheritance!

Paul adds, however, "provided we suffer with him in order that we may also be glorified with him" (v. 17). When Christ came to earth on our behalf, he did not get any glory. The only time he was ever lifted up in any way was when he was nailed to a cross. The throngs cheered for him, but only when they mistakenly thought he was going to overthrow the Roman Empire. Everyone in Jerusalem knew he died like a common criminal; only a handful knew he was raised from the dead and ascended into heaven. This Jesus, who invites us to join him as brothers and sisters in God's family, also calls us to join him in obscurity and suffering: "If any man would come after me," Jesus said, "let him deny himself and take up his cross and follow me" (Mt 16:24).

Being Jesus' brother or sister, then, means sharing everything with him. It means joining him in obedience and suffering as well as in his glorious reward. "Whoever does the will of my Father in heaven is my brother, and sister, and mother," Jesus said (Mt 12:50), and this made perfect sense to his first-century listeners who knew that you could not contest the patriarch's authority and still consider yourself part of the family.

## Needed: Character

What does it take to do the will of the Father? It takes *courage* to join a family that is misunderstood by the world. It takes *discipline* to accomplish the tasks God has set out for his children. It takes *vision* to overcome inevitable problems and to see what God is doing in the lives of his children. It takes *endurance* to stick with your brothers and sisters when it would be so much easier to go your own way. Above all, it takes *love* to hold God's family together and to reach out and invite others to join it— tender, tough, sacrificial, radical love.

In a word, it takes *character* to do God's will—and, wonder of wonders, Christ's character is what God offers us when we timidly say we would like to be part of his family. Paul writes that those whom God chooses for his family members he makes "conformed to the image of his Son" (Rom 8:29)—he gives them character qualities like those of their elder brother, Jesus.

He does this through the work of the Holy Spirit, his representative in our hearts. "We all . . . beholding the glory of the Lord, are being changed into his likeness from one degree of glory to another; for this comes from the Lord who is the Spirit" (2 Cor 3:18). The Spirit writes Jesus' own character traits on our hearts: "love, joy, peace, patience, kindness, goodness, faithfulness, gentleness, self-control" (Gal 5:22-23).

After adopting us and making us like Christ, God invites us to claim our inheritance—the same glorious reward claimed by the triumphant Jesus after his resurrection. Jesus is eager to share his inheritance with us: "The glory which thou hast given me I have given to them" (Jn 17:22), he said of his disciples. He will not take the spotlight alone. Instead, "when Christ who is our life appears, then you also will appear with him in glory" (Col 3:4). When Jesus Christ reveals himself in glory to the whole world, he will bring us—his brothers and sisters—with him to share his glory eternally.

The more I learn about Jesus Christ, the more I love him. I realize he is worthy of all my adoration, devotion and praise; he is worthy of my whole life's service. He is a giver, not a thief; an owner, not a hired hand; a father, not a taskmaster. He wants to make me part of his family and give me the character qualities I need in order to live obediently, successfully and happily, now and forever. He wants to have a personal relationship with me that will last eternally, because his heart overflows with love for me.

If you do not know this side of Jesus Christ, God longs to reveal it to you. He wants to adopt you into his family. All you need to do is say, "Lord, I am a sinner who could never earn entrance into your family. But because your perfect Son Jesus died for me, I am eligible for adoption. I want to be part of your family. Thank you for taking me in."

If you do that, God will take you into his family immediately. He won't say, "Wait a few years until your character is more like my Son's," because he knows that character qualities develop best inside the family, not outside it. He will take you just as you are; and with infinite love, patience and gentleness he will begin shaping you. He will send you the Holy Spirit as a living adoption certificate, and you will know that your status as God's child is legal, permanent and binding.

Many secular thinkers know that character development is one of the most important tasks facing this generation. Without it, our nation, our families and millions of individuals are in grave danger; with it, strength and success are still possible. But character development is a difficult, even grim, task when undertaken with no more than firm resolution and gritted teeth.

Character qualities are more easily caught than taught. Like young plants, they develop best in a warm, nurturing atmosphere.

That is exactly what God offers: the best possible example of character, Jesus Christ; and the best possible school for character, the fellowship of his own family. Today is not too soon to take that first small step of courage and say, "Yes, Lord, I want to be like Jesus. Please take me into your family and love me into your likeness."

# Christes In You

## by Charles Price

What is the simplest yet most profound discovery that any Christian can make? Surely it is this: that God has actually given us himself. He comes to live in us and be our strength and make us more like him.

Charles Price shows how God's presence, his laws and his daily provision will satisfy us in the frenetic pace of modern life. With clarity and warmth he explains some of the Bible's less well-known symbols, and so awakens us to a whole new understanding of what it is for Christ to live in us.

K
**Kingsway Publications**

# God's Passion for You

## by Sam Storms

God delights in you. Does it sound too good to be true?
You know you're not good enough. You know you
can't earn his love. Yet he loves you with unwavering
passion.

Using examples from Scripture, church history and
today, Sam Storms reveals the depths of God's
pleasure in his people – a pleasure that springs from
his very own nature and purposes. God does not wait
for us to change before he will love us; yet his love is
the very best agent for change in us, once we have let it
take root.

Let God's passion for you ignite your passion for
him, and for those who do not yet know the riches of
God's love.

With a foreword by Mike Bickle.

SAM STORMS is the associate pastor at Metro Christian
Fellowship, Kansas City, and a graduate of Dallas
Theological Seminary.

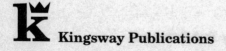

**Kingsway Publications**

# Stop the Rollercoaster –
# I Want to Get Off!

## by Ronald Dunn

Are you tired of living on a spiritual rollercoaster? Is your climb to the 'mountain-top experience' always followed by a plunge into the valley of despair and disappointment?

Too many Christians think that this type of existence is normal for the believer. But as *physical* growth is normal for the body, so *spiritual* growth is normal for the spirit.

Using the book of Joshua as his basis, Ronald Dunn shows us that we must not only cross the Red Sea *out* of Egypt, but cross the Jordan *into* Canaan. Then the promises of God in Scripture become realities in our daily lives.

RONALD DUNN left the pastorate in 1975 to devote himself to a worldwide ministry of preaching and teaching. He is the President of Lifestyle Ministries and he and his wife, Kaye, live in Irving, Texas. He is the author of the acclaimed *Don't Just Stand There, Pray Something!*

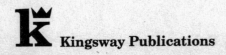

**Kingsway Publications**

# Stop Trying to Live for Jesus
## ... Let Him Live Through You

**by Charles Price**

We want to dedicate our lives to God's service, and rightly so. Yet how easy it is to come under the burden of attempting the impossible: a life lived in our own strength rather than in the power available to us in Christ.

If you want to break out of the cycle of trying, failing, and trying again, this book is for you.

CHARLES PRICE is Principal of Capernwray Bible School in Carnforth, a board member of the Keswick Convention and a popular conference speaker and Bible teacher.

**K** Kingsway Publications

# Will God Heal Me?

## by Ronald Dunn

As a pastor, Ronald Dunn has prayed for the sick and
seen them healed; and he has prayed and seen them
die. There have been times when he has known a
special assurance that healing would come, and others
when events have been almost impossible to
understand.

Explanations abound, for we all want to know why
God doesn't always heal. We are told to have more
faith, to confess our sins, or to claim our inheritance.
But such explanations usually add to the burdens of
both the sick and those who care for them. They are
*partly* correct, but there is no greater danger to truth
than *partial* truth.

This book will take the pressure off those who do not
feel they are allowed to be ill. It is replete with true
stories, but these are examined in the light of the
Bible's teaching, lest we be eager to turn experience
into doctrine.

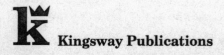

**Kingsway Publications**